Contents Copyright © 2023

Copying and distributing portions of this book without permission or without citing the source Is a violation of copyright. Sales of materials without permission is not permitted. To become eligible to sell this book you must become an approved Facilitator.

GLOSSARY

Text Version	Pages 3 – 19
Day 1	Pages 20 – 36
Day 2	Pages 37 – 63
Day 3	Pages 64 – 90
Day 4	Pages 91 – 121
Day 5	Pages 122 – 149
Recovery Plan – 6 Month	Pages 152 – 181
Recovery Plan – 1 Year	Pages 182 – 210
Recovery Plan – 3 Year	Pages 211 – 239
Extra Facilitator Info + How to Become a Facilitator + Authors Note	Pages 240 - 247

Welcome to Radical Recovery Peer Support!

If you are reading this, you may be interested in or have been invited to participate in a Radical Recovery Peer Support group. Therefore, it is worth mentioning that the driving factor of the group is robust participation. We believe that participation increases engagement and reduces the monotony of only having the group Facilitator present material.

All participation in the group is voluntary, however in some instances a person may be mandated to participate. Even in this scenario, the person has the ability to refuse participation which may result in some other option or consequence for them. This is based on their situation and has nothing to do with the group process. Because participation is voluntary, we cannot be sure from one group to another how many people will participate, causing differences from group to group of how much material any one person will present.

Our program offers a certificate of participation and a certificate of completion. People may need a certificate to receive some benefit or to avert a consequence. To receive either certificate, a person will have different participation requirements. Only a certificate of completion will allow a participant to take the next step of becoming a group Facilitator.

Group Facilitators must be able to highly identify with the program. This means that for all the questions other than the ones labeled "how does this passage connect to…," the Facilitator must be able to answer 85% of the questions. Everyone can participate by taking turns reading the material and answering "how does this passage connect to…," but those who are unable to complete at least 85% of the questions may struggle to answer them in group which is why only those seeking a certificate of completion to become Facilitators will answer the questions during group.

While many people may participate in the group for different reasons, we encourage everyone to participate as if they are trying to earn a certificate of completion because it will make the group more dynamic and Peer Supported. The biggest hurdle is determining if you believe you can answer 85% of the questions. Hopefully you will receive a question list or the book a couple weeks before group begins. If that fails, there is at least a week or two between the first group session where no questions are answered, and the second session. We suggest using that time to look over the questions and determine if you can answer 85% of the questions. To earn a certificate of completion your books answers must be checked for quality and completeness.

About This Program:

Radical Recovery Peer Support is a program that utilizes Peer Support to help individuals achieve wellness and personal growth. The author of the program uses first-person inspirational passages to draw parallels between concepts and recovery. The Program Involves group sessions that can be done either in-person or online.

For the group programs, we have three options. This book/group is about recovery from a criminal past. The Second is a general wellness and personal growth group which is simply called Radical Recovery Peer Support. There is also a group with a focus on higher or continued education called RRPS-University.

Over the course of five sessions each group covers important concepts like the Linear Growth Model and Parallel Recovery Concepts. It Also Focuses on the nine Recovery Fundamentals which include principles like Honesty, Trust, Acceptance, Hope, Personal Responsibility, Self-Advocacy, and others. How each group presents the concepts and fundamentals is unique.

The Linear Growth Model recognizes that while growth and recovery are not always linear, putting in effort does often lead to progress over time. Growth may appear uneven, with periods of progress and periods of struggle. However, making consistent efforts through programs like Radical Recovery Peer Support can help us move closer to our hope of achieving stability and wellness.

RRPS is a Cognitive Behavioral Therapy. It is such because the description of the Concepts and Fundamentals, as well as the person first descriptions of the recovery journey address beliefs, thoughts, and feelings commonly experienced in a specific but large audience. Each program addresses thoughts, beliefs, and feelings that held the author back and provides a solution of improving our thoughts, beliefs, and control over our feelings by getting more aligned with positive expressions of Recovery Concepts and Fundamentals.

Examples of how this is done includes changing thoughts for people with criminal history's such as "Only my failures matter," to "I have hope even though its tougher with a record." Changing thoughts of "All probation officers are out to get me" to many of them want to help." Reduces Dichotomous thinking by encouraging the view that its not all black or white or one or the other, but that there are levels of growth on a continuum and a new start can be made at any time.

The programs also incorporate themes of Rational Emotive Therapy in the different events emphasized in each program. With more general distressing circumstances in the original RRPS, to more specific events such as educational neglect in RRPS - University, and the stigma of having a criminal record in RRPS -Liberation, to our beliefs about these issues, and the consequences for results of those beliefs. The group also utilizes themes of Reality Therapy is its emphasis on exercising choice and personal responsibility.

The program also utilizes a wide variety of homework questions that are done outside of group (common of CBT programs) which reinforce the goals of the program. Each Passage that relates an experience based on a Concept or Fundamental usually focuses on a change in thinking that improves each outcome.

Schedule

Session one covers an introduction to the Linear Growth Model, the Parallel Recovery Concepts, and the 9 Recovery Fundamentals.

Session two Covers the three Parallel Recovery Concepts.

Session three covers the first three fundamentals of Honesty, Trust, And Acceptance.

Session four covers Hope, Personal Responsibility, and Self Advocacy.

Session five covers Support, Purpose, and Self -actualization..

Goals

This curriculum emphasizes balanced linear growth through development of 9 Recovery Fundamentals and 3 Parallel Recovery Concepts that occur alongside each of the 9 Fundamentals. The goals of this program are based on the Fundamentals of Recovery and the Recovery Concepts and are to teach participants how to:

1. Learn the importance of and how to perform Self-Care
2. Learn to develop a Recovery Plan to take recovery to greater heights (Recovery Planning)
3. learn that while participating in recovery we are at every moment a mentor and a model of recovery behavior
4. overcome challenges, handle stressful or difficult situations and/or troubling thoughts, achieve personal growth and wellness, and live a self-directed life

Goals One, Two, and Three, represent the three Parallel Recovery Concepts of Self-Care, Recovery Planning, and Mentoring - Respectively. Goal four represents the result of successfully incorporating the 9 Recovery Fundamentals into daily life in addition to the Recovery Concepts. On a graph it looks like:

Figure 1:

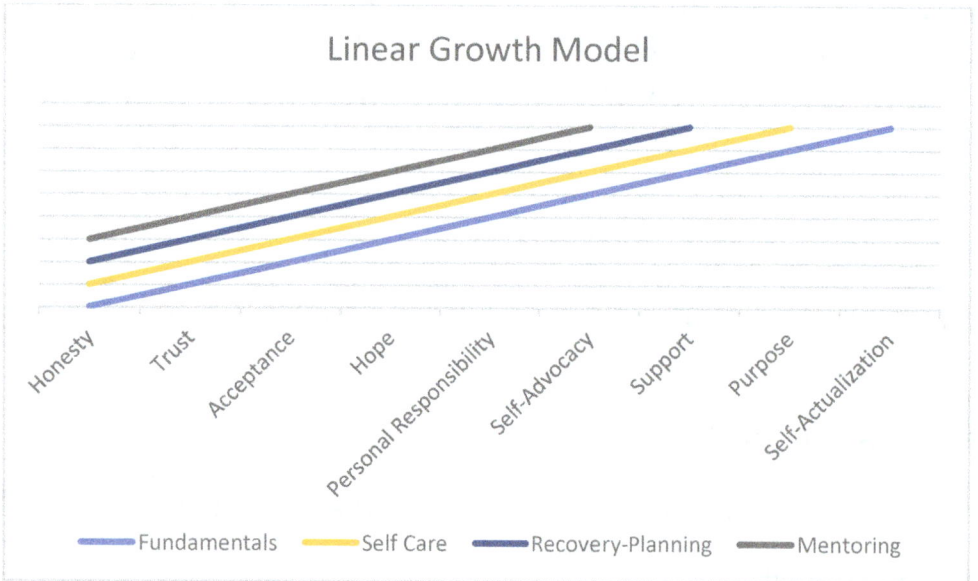

*Tip: Notice that the graph begins with linear growth along the line representing the Fundamentals of Recovery. By implementing the 3 Parallel Recovery Concepts of Self-Care, Recovery Planning, and Mentoring, outcomes and the growth line can be continuously shifted upward to higher levels of growth.

Not only does this program emphasize that every step we take along the path to personal growth and freedom is a moment that encourages others in our society, but it points out that growth is actually fuller and more complete when we remember to care for ourselves, plan for recovery, and when we help others like us, we see that recovery is possible.

From the Better Days workbook passage *'Creating Change':* "Mahatma Gandhi, the great Indian spiritual leader, said, 'Be the change you want to see in the world.' Gregorio Lewis, Author of Better Days Restates this point saying "I say that first I must change myself into the person I want to be."

The words from the passage *'Creating Change'* and Mahatma Gandhi indicate that by learning to focus on our personal experience of growth and change, the world will change in our direction, as we model the behaviors we want to see in the world.

Many programs say that **giving back** and **helping others** with the same problems as we have experienced is a sort of final step. The reasoning behind this program and in Peer Support in general is that showing recovery is possible occurs alongside every stage in the process and our actions create a lasting impact.

In addition, many people who have been successful in recovery say that

- giving back
- taking commitments to support others, and
- remembering that they are an example of recovery in their communities

helped them the most in their recovery.

The 9 Fundamentals of Recovery

Recovery Fundamentals are a set of characteristics that we can use to gauge the strength of our recovery and include but are not limited to:

1. Honesty
2. Trust
3. Acceptance
4. Hope
5. Personal Responsibility
6. Self-Advocacy
7. Support
8. Purpose
9. Self-Actualization

A breakdown of the fundamentals listed first can cause difficulty with fundamentals listed last. The Fundamentals of Recovery are qualities we want to encourage in participants of this program. It is important to remember the quote from Mahatma Ghandi that we should "be the change we want to see in the world." Because we are always Mentors, it is vitally important that we demonstrate the Recovery Fundamentals because our effort, or lack of effort will impact others.

The Linear Growth Model

Growth often does not occur linearly, although many of us wish it did.

What it Usually Looks Like

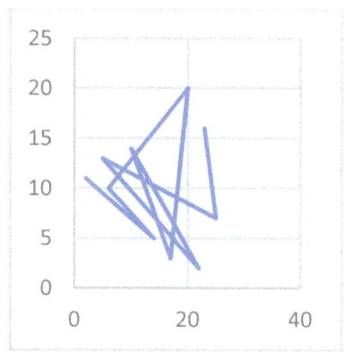

Our Hopes

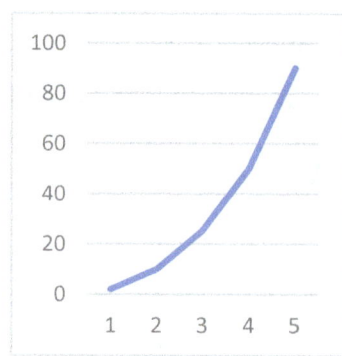

What it Could Look Like

Many recovery programs emphasize that growth is non-linear. However Radical Recovery Peer Support believes that over-emphasizing the non-linear nature of growth is self-defeating. While we acknowledge growth is non-linear, we also believe that in most cases, we do make progress when we put in effort. To over emphasize the non-linear nature of growth tends to give people an excuse to use, such as that there is no guarantee that if they work hard they will grow.

With all the twists and turns and ups and downs of recovery, it can be hard to even tell if growth is occurring. By putting the same amount of effort and care into each of the Recovery Fundamentals, we will get more consistent results than if we were to put all our efforts in one Fundamental.

Because our own actions and behaviors change and impact the world around us, it is common that when we start exhibiting a better relationship with the Recovery Fundamentals, we will experience a mirror effect from the world. We may sometimes wonder why it seems we receive exaggerated reactions or displays of the Fundamentals directed back at us from society but can understand that this may be connected to our own inconsistent demonstrations of the Fundamentals.

The Linear Growth Model gets its name from the idea that

1. Growth is usually Non-Linear
2. we want to put consistent effort into each of the 9 Fundamentals which will result in more, but not all, consistent experiences in our lives.
3. When developed inconsistently with this format, inconsistent and unexpected outcomes may occur.
4. When developed in the order listed previously, each of the 9 Recovery Fundamentals assists in the cultivation and growth of the other Fundamentals.
5. When Utilizing the Parallel Recovery Concepts in conjunction with the Recovery Fundamentals, we can shift our results to a better outcome

False Sense of Security:

When we experience success at Recovery Concepts or the later Fundamentals, particularly starting with Personal Responsibility through Self-Advocacy, Support, and Purpose, we may be lulled into a false sense of security that we are doing well despite shortfalls related to the earlier Fundamentals.

We encourage that no matter our level of success with later Fundamentals, we take a look at how the earlier fundamentals show up for us. Gaps in our development may lead to blind spots that may damage our recovery.

Why We Present the Fundamentals of Recovery and the 3 Parallel Recovery Concepts in This Order

Even though Parallel Recovery Concepts occur throughout our Recovery, there are many reasons for each component that if we do not take proper care of each Recovery Fundamental and Parallel Recovery Concept, we will not unlock the full growth potential of incorporating Recovery Concepts or later Fundamentals into our lives.

We give examples of how neglecting components of the Recovery Concepts and Fundamentals of Recovery leads to a breakdown of the transition to the other components:

Recovery Concepts: This group process and other methods of Recovery can be really hard on us emotionally, mentally, and physically; therefore, it is important that we are kind to ourselves and benefit from this process. From the very beginning of an attempt to better ourselves, such as participating in this group, it will be important to maintain the Recovery Concepts of Self-Care, Recovery Planning, and Mentorship. Right from the beginning it is important to:

- Have a self-care plan, acknowledge the difficulty of this process, and create positive experiences to look forward to
- develop a Recovery plan involving the desired outcome and benefit of this process,
- and recognize that our participation in this process can either help or hinder the recovery of other participants.

Honesty: if we are in fear of what someone will find out about our secrets, harm done to others, past crimes and the things that make us feel guilt, shame, or fear of persecution, we will not know what we can <u>trust</u> others with.

Trust: If we cannot trust ourselves or are not aware of who we can Trust or what systems are working for us and not against us, we will have a hard time finding <u>acceptance</u> of our situation.

Acceptance: If we can't accept our current situation or past experiences and are constantly suffering from them or if someone or some force has an uncomfortable level of control over our lives, we will have a hard time recognizing things we can <u>hope</u> for.

Hope: If we don't have hope and are not propelled by our desire to achieve a hoped-for outcome, the natural inclination is to be unmotivated about our personal responsibilities. If we can't get satisfaction by working on our hopes, we often fail to develop and perform personal responsibilities.

Personal Responsibilities: if we are lacking in fulfilling our personal responsibilities, we often face resistance from others when we self-advocate for ourselves because we have less basis to show that we are capable.

Self-Advocacy: If we fail to effectively advocate for ourselves through means of showing that our capabilities or progress make us a good fit for certain endeavors, or if we advocate for ourselves for that which provides outcomes inconsistent with our recovery, or if we advocate to the wrong people, among other things, we may not get adequate support.

Support: A Significant outcome of working through the Fundamentals of Recovery leading up to support, is that we find ourselves in the best position to begin offering support.

It takes support to fulfil BIG goals. If we do not look for support or accept support from the right people, we will have a hard time achieving our goals. With the added effort it takes to achieve goals without support we have a hard time finding our purpose because everything feels like it is a struggle. Often, things that seem more natural or easier for us, or areas we get the most support, are also area's excellent to find purpose.

Purpose: Without a purpose with which to gauge our progress or put our efforts, we often feel like we are repeating a pattern that rarely changes, or that there is no perceivable pattern but rather instability or lack of focus. Finding and incorporating a purpose into our lives leads to <u>self-actualization</u>, a feeling that we are fulfilling our unique potential

Self-Actualization: This Fundamental of Recovery is often considered a final stage of development. However, to maintain this stage we must continue to put sufficient and equal amounts of effort into all the Fundamentals of Recovery. Also, the Parallel Recovery Concepts must be maintained.

What Mentors Need to Know

Self-Care:

Self-care is any healthy & direct action we take to feel better. Sometimes we need to use Self-Care to respond to stressors, or triggering events, or when we feel like we are in crises. Self-Care that might work normally may not work as well under very difficult conditions.

*Tip for dealing with stressors: One suggestion for how to deal with especially difficult situations is to put more time and effort into the things we usually do to make us feel better.

Really good Self-Care is often planned. Planning Self-Care before we feel unwell has benefits such as having something to look forward to, or helping us not forget Self-Care. Because of this, it is often included in recovery planning.

Examples of Self-Care

- *Remembering our boundaries and what we will or will not do*
- *Spending time with family and friends*
- *Getting enough sleep*
- *Being of service to others*
- *Writing a gratitude list*
- *Taking breaks*

Stressors, burnout, vicarious trauma, poor time management, and compassion fatigue are common reasons we provide Self-Care for ourselves.

Recovery Planning:

Recovery planning is self-determined but often includes friends and family, supporters, or community leaders. Recovery planning is done with the collaboration of individuals involved and utilizes recovery capital.

A Recovery Plan
- *Is based on self-determination*
- *Identifies strengths of the individual and takes inventory of Recovery Capital*
- *Identifies goals, challenges, action steps, and date of completion*
- *May involve support from others and connection to community resources and leadership.*

In a table it looks like:

Goal	Strengths & Recovery Capital	Obstacles	Action Steps	Date of Completion
Get Masters Degree	<ul><li>Have a: bachelors degree</li><li>Time: Am on Disability and am self employed</li><li>Experienced with: online courses</li></ul>	Classes are condensed so more is required in a shorter time.	<ul><li>Clear agenda for first week</li><li>Start each day with school first</li><li>Complete all assignments before recreation</li></ul>	August 10th 2025

Recovery plans need to be evaluated and measured for progress. Criteria for evaluation should come from the person creating the plan and should be considered before action, if possible.

Mentoring:

Mentoring is a constant ongoing process and occurs in situations where we present both the best or worst aspects of ourselves. We never know just what kind of impact we will have on others. Remember the words of Mahatma Gandhi – "be the change you want to see in the world." One way to effect change is through Mentoring.

- Mentoring provides an opportunity to be there for a person in a way that supports them in both the best of times and the worst
- A good mentor will respect each person's unique approach to recovery
- A Mentor utilizes self-disclosure in a way that does not compete with but rather informs an individual of shared experiences
- A Mentor should be primarily focused on the person they are mentoring; only sharing about themselves or their experiences when it would be a benefit to the mentee
- Mentoring is constant and ongoing, and occurs in situations where we present both the best or worst aspects of ourselves
- We never know just what kind of impact we will have on others

Honesty:

Many of us have Baggage. In recovery, we may resist new healthy behaviors and thoughts. This may often stem from a lack of honesty about three factors, 1: that they have been hurt and/or 2: that they have hurt themselves or others, and 3: the nature of the severity of the hurt.

It is important to acknowledge:

- if we are not honest within ourselves about how we have been hurt, hurt ourselves or others, or the severity, we may repeat unfavorable experiences.

Trust:

There are different levels of trust - We can have trust in:

- a specific person or people that we trust
- in the systems we are in such as our governments, legal system, or system of wellness or therapy
- self-trust; <u>trusting that we have our own best interests in mind</u>.

Within these is determining who we can rely on, who we cannot, and what we can share with others.

*Tip – Self-disclosure: It is important to remember

- we never need to share something that would make us uncomfortable
- there is more we can share with others than something that would make us uncomfortable
- it is different to share things we want to keep private versus our hopes, goals, and stresses
- there is no guarantee what we say will remain confidential

Acceptance:

Each person is subject to different degrees of unforeseen circumstances, restrictions, rules, and regulations. For the most part, these obstacles depend on our situation, can be temporary, or can be changed with support. While we must deal with these situations while they occur, we can find ways to have hope within them and have Better Days.

*Tip – Trauma/Grief Informed: Many people will report that there are things that they cannot or will not accept. This is okay, remind them that they can still work on other Fundamentals and that there is a difference between 1: accepting that an event took place and 2: accepting an event into our lives and our space.

Hope:

If we are struggling to find hope, it will often become easier the longer we commit to recovery and through more time between distressing events. Also, <u>actively seek out inspiration</u> by:

- talking to supporters about what is giving our supporters hope
- making lists of things that give us hope
- reading recovery stories
- list their own dreams, and if possible, communicate them to someone

Personal Responsibility:

Some situations may be out of our control or cause discomfort for us. If we are having a hard time fulfilling responsibilities because of obstacles, things outside our control, or things we need or are worried about; we can ask how much control we have over these situations, and if we are doing everything we can within the control we have.

Personal Responsibility Continued -

To get back on track we can follow a Recovery Plan that involves:

- A daily plan
- A plan of things we need to do every now and then
- A plan for achieving big goals

Plans should include a way to provide for ourselves and elements of Self-Care

If we are developing a Recovery Plan, it is important to first list things we struggle with, things that need the most attention, or that create new responsibilities for us. A Recovery Plan is a way to familiarize ourselves with our objectives and requirements and decide how things need to be done.

Personal Responsibility may involve creating goals that improve our lives and our success. For information on how to help someone with their goals, refer to the section of the RRPS Mentors Guide titled Motivational Interviewing & Recovery Planning.

Self-Advocacy:

Sometimes people may feel they have lost their right or ability to advocate for themselves, or that they have lost control of their lives. Each person has the right to advocate for themselves for the same public benefits and treatment common to their society no matter what the state of their lives.

*Tip – if a person is having a hard time gaining support through self-advocacy, communicate that

- our chances of getting support increase the longer we maintain continued effort with the Recovery Fundamentals that precede this step, especially Personal Responsibility.

- we can believe in ourselves and practice advocating by making a list of goals we think will get the most support and advocating for each item on the list.

Support:

"It takes support to fulfill BIG goals. If we do not look for support or accept support from the right people, we will have a tougher time achieving our goals."

If we lack support, developing a strong support system benefits from:

- being mutually supportive to others
- doing everything within our control to maintain our personal definition of wellness
- becoming active in the community, a support group, school, or other area like employment
- having several supporters so someone will always be available, and we do not overburden anyone

Purpose:

Once we have maintained progress relevant to our interests and security, are more empowered, and have support, we may find that other people are an extension of ourselves or that we have integrated a cause into our lives.

We may also find that

- human rights,
- dignity,

and

- freedom

become important to us.

Self-Actualization:

Self-actualization is all about reaching the true potential of our unique selves. Once we have reached our full potential, we may find that we are freer and more capable. Often, people at this level of development begin to have a deeper connection with where they believe they fit in the universe, existence, and in relation to other people or their concept of a higher power.

In the *Allegory of the Cave* "Plato's Republic," the principal character in the story returns to people that were still "disillusioned" to help them find a better way. For most this is a natural inclination by this stage of recovery, to show others a brighter future. The Parallel Recovery Concept of Mentorship has carried many individuals' recoveries to particularly new heights. Consider the shift in the growth demonstrated in the Linear Growth Model due to the Parallel Recovery Concepts and Mentorship.

Presentation Process

The slides that can be read in the workbook or PowerPoint will be divided between all those wishing to receive a certificate of participation or completion, including participation from the facilitators. The Facilitators will start by explaining why we request full participation and the reward of either a certificate of completion or participation. The Information on participation requirements is on page two underneath the table of contents.

The Facilitators will read the first two slides of the first presentation. After that, all slides will be divided up between the participants. The exceptions to this are the slides in the first session's presentation following the slide title "Why We Present the Recovery Fundamentals and Parallel Recovery Concepts in this Order." These slides sometimes contain more than one Fundamental or Concept and there will be a different reader for each of these.

At the end of each session, the Facilitator will read the last slide that conveys information related to the upcoming session. After this, the remainder of the time will be spent on open discussion of the day's session. For session one this will be the full span of 2 hours, for the remaining session it will be the span of 3 hours.

The remaining sessions also have sections titled 'How does this passage connect or relate to the concept or fundamental.' These questions entail a short response that should connect the passage read just before this question to the Recovery Concept or Fundamental being discussed at the time. Everyone has the capability to answer these questions so everyone desiring a certificate of participation or completion will answer these including the facilitator, unless facilitator participation means some participants will not have the chance to participate.

Participation points will not be lost for these questions if there were not enough questions for everyone to get a chance to participate. A participation sheet will be provided which specifies how many participation points a person will need in each category of participation. For those who have not had a chance to answer these questions, they will have an opportunity to revisit them at the end of the group.

Sessions 2 – 5 also have many short questions. There are usually 3 questions for each passage. These are divided between all those seeking a certificate of completion and the Facilitators. These questions are not required to be answered by those seeking a certificate of participation.

The Facilitator will not participate or read unless there are fewer than 5 people attempting a certificate of completion, in which case, only participating when they have the least amount of participation compared to those seeking a certificate. Participants can choose when they would like to participate in order to get the right amount of participation points, however when some of them are close to full points, the facilitator will begin asking specific people to participate if a participant has the least amount of participation.

If participants do not have a response to a particular question, the Facilitator will step in and answer the question. If participants did not get enough participation points from this question-and-answer section, we can allow them to answer other questions from the session at the end as a revisitation.

To revisit a question requires them to have completed enough of their answers to share them and receive the required completion points. This might be useful for participants that did not complete enough of their questions before the group where the questions they did answer in the book were answered by other participants. Even if the participant did not complete a question before group, we can allow them to develop a quick answer on the spot if they are able.

Once the presentation process is over for the session, we allow the rest of the time to be open discussion starting with the facilitator asking the group if they have any questions, allowing participants to ask questions here. Next, we will do a check in, asking the group how they are doing with the concepts or fundamentals covered in the session. Once 2 hours have elapsed for session one, or three hours for all other sessions, the session is complete.

This is how the group will be Facilitated.

P.s.

On the last page of each day's session, the text will also point out what needs to be completed before the next day's session. All assignments discussed on these pages will be shared by participants in breakout rooms if the group is online, or with the person sitting next to them if done in person.

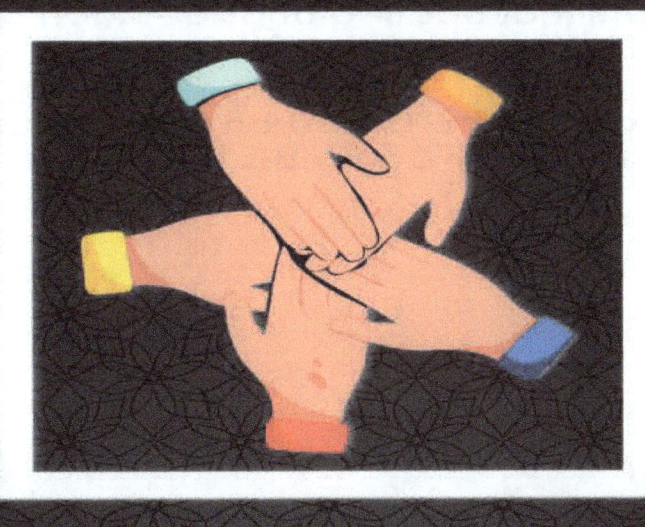

Radical Recovery Peer Support- Liberation

Day 1

This curriculum emphasizes balanced linear growth through the development of 9 Recovery Fundamentals and three Parallel Recovery Concepts that occur alongside each of the 9 Fundamentals.

The goals of this program are based on the Fundamentals of Recovery and the Recovery Concepts. They are:

Learn the importance of and how to perform Self-Care

Learn to develop a Recovery Plan to take recovery to greater heights (Recovery Planning)

Overcome challenges or troubling thoughts, handle stressful or difficult situations, achieve personal growth and wellness, and live a self-directed life

Learn that while participating in recovery we are at every moment a mentor and a model of recovery behavior

From the Better Days workbook passage 'Creating Change': "Mahatma Gandhi, the great Indian spiritual leader, said, 'Be the change you want to see in the world.'

Gregorio Lewis, Author of Better Days restates this point by saying "I say that first I must change myself into the person I want to be."

The words from the passage *'Creating Change'* and Mahatma Gandhi indicate that by learning to focus on our personal experience of growth and change, the world will change in our direction, as we model the behaviors we want to see in the world.

Many programs say that **giving back** and **helping others** with the same problems as we have experienced is a sort of final step. The reasoning of this program and in Peer Support in general is that showing recovery is possible occurs alongside every stage in the process and our actions create a lasting impact.

In addition, many people who have been successful in recovery say that

- giving back
- taking commitments to support others, and
- remembering that they are an example of recovery in their communities

helped them the most in their recovery.

The 9 Recovery Fundamentals

Recovery Fundamentals are a set of characteristics that we can use to gauge the strength of our recovery and include but are not limited to:

- Honesty
- Trust
- Acceptance
- Hope
- Personal Responsibility
- Self-Advocacy
- Support
- Purpose
- Self-Actualization

A breakdown of the Fundamentals listed first can cause difficulty with the Fundamentals listed last

NOTES:

Parallel Recovery Concepts

Self Care

Recovery Planning

Mentoring

Growth often does not occur linearly, although many of us wish it did – Imagine if you knew X amount of effort led to Y amount of growth!

- We often hope growth would look like this

- What it usually looks like

The Linear Growth Model

Growth we can aim for

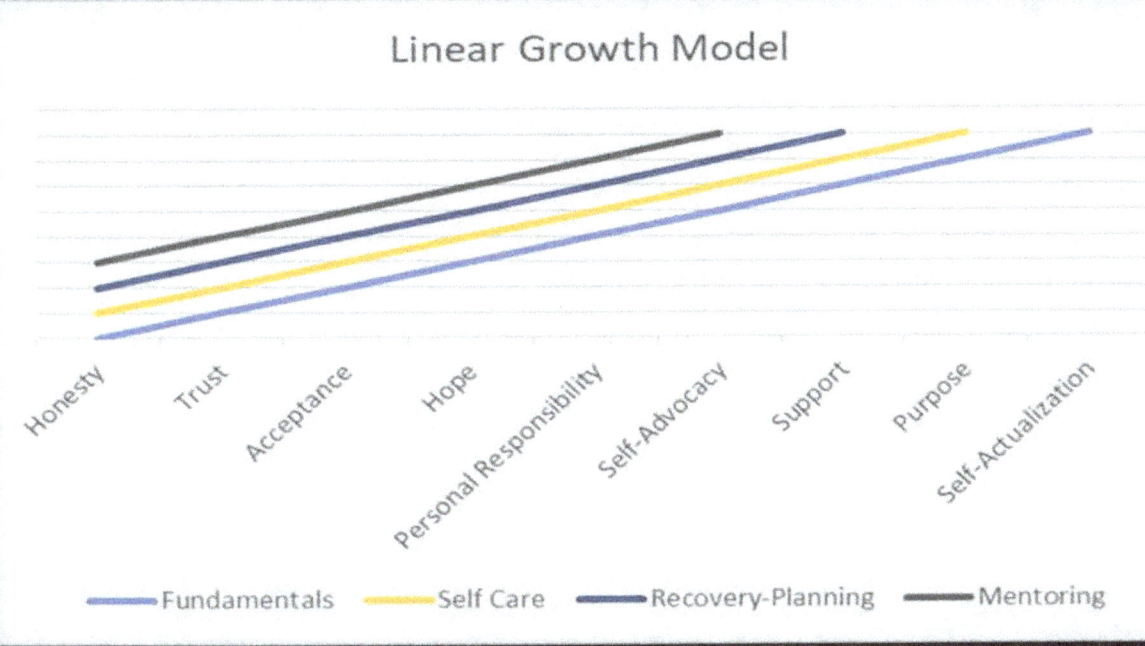

The Linear Growth Model (Continued)

The Linear Growth Model gets its name from the idea that

1. Growth is usually Non-Linear

2. We want to put consistent effort into each of the 9 Fundamentals which will result in more, but not all, consistent experiences in our lives.

3. When developed inconsistently with this format, inconsistent and unexpected outcomes may occur.

4. When developed in the order listed previously, each of the 9 Recovery Fundamentals assists in the cultivation and growth of the other Fundamentals.

5. When Utilizing the Parallel Recovery Concepts in conjunction with the Recovery Fundamentals, we can shift our results to a better outcome

The Linear Growth Model (Continued)

With all the twists and turns and ups and downs of recovery, it can be hard to even tell if growth is occurring. By putting the same amount of effort and care into each of the Recovery Fundamentals, we will get more consistent results than if we were to put all our efforts in one Fundamental.

Because our own actions and behaviors change and impact the world around us, it is common that when we start exhibiting a better relationship with the Recovery Fundamentals, we will experience a mirror effect from the world. We may sometimes wonder why it seems we receive exaggerated reactions or displays of the Fundamentals directed back at us from society but can understand that this may be connected to our own inconsistent demonstrations of the Fundamentals.

False Sense of Security

When we experience success at Recovery Concepts or the later Fundamentals, particularly starting with Personal Responsibility through Self-Advocacy, Support, and Purpose, we may be lulled into a false sense of security that we are doing well despite shortfalls related to the earlier Fundamentals.

We encourage that no matter our level of success with later Fundamentals, we take a look at how the earlier fundamentals show up for us. Gaps in our development may lead to blind spots that may damage our recovery.

Why We Present the Recovery Fundamentals and Parallel Recovery Concepts in This Order

There are many reasons that if we do not take proper care of each Recovery Fundamental and Parallel Recovery Concept, we will not unlock the full growth potential of incorporating Recovery Concepts or Fundamentals into our lives.

We give examples of how neglecting components of the Recovery Concepts and Fundamentals leads to a breakdown of the transition to the other components:

Recovery Concepts:

This group process and other methods of Recovery can be hard on us emotionally, mentally, and physically; therefore, it is important that we are kind to ourselves and benefit from this process.

From the very beginning of an attempt to better ourselves, such as participating in this group, it will be important to maintain the Recovery Concepts of Self-Care, Recovery Planning, and Mentorship.

Right from the beginning it is important to:

- Have a self-care plan, acknowledge the difficulty of this process, and create positive experiences to look forward to

- develop a Recovery plan involving the desired outcome and benefit of this process,

- and recognize that our participation in this process can either help or hinder the recovery of other participants.

Recovery Fundamentals:

Honesty: if we are in fear of what someone will find out about our secrets, harm done to others, past crimes, and the things that make us feel guilt, shame, or fear of persecution, we will not know what we can trust others with.

Trust: If we cannot trust ourselves or are not aware of who we can Trust or what systems are working for us and not against us, we will have a hard time finding acceptance of our situation.

Acceptance: If we can't accept our current situation or past experiences and are constantly suffering from them or if someone or some force has an uncomfortable level of control over our lives, we will have a hard time recognizing things we can hope for.

Recovery Fundamentals:

Hope: If we don't have any hope and are not propelled by our desire to achieve a hoped-for outcome, the natural inclination is to be unmotivated about our personal responsibilities. If we can't get satisfaction by working on our hopes, we often fail to develop and perform personal responsibilities.

Personal Responsibilities: if we are lacking in fulfilling our personal responsibilities, we often face resistance from others when we self-advocate for ourselves because we have less basis to show that we are capable.

Self-Advocacy: If we fail to effectively advocate for ourselves through means of showing that our capabilities or progress make us a good fit for certain endeavors, or if we advocate for ourselves for that which provides outcomes inconsistent with our recovery, or if we advocate to the wrong people, among other things, we may not get adequate support.

Recovery Fundamentals:

Support: A Significant outcome of working through the Recovery Fundamentals leading up to support, is that we find ourselves in the best position to begin offering support.

It takes support to fulfil BIG goals. If we do not look for support or accept support from the right people, we may have a hard time achieving our goals. With the added effort it takes to achieve goals without support, we have a hard time finding our purpose because of the effort and struggle. Often, things that seem more natural or easier for us, or areas where we get the most support, are also the area's excellent to find purpose.

Recovery Fundamentals:

Purpose: Without a purpose with which to gauge our progress or put our efforts, we often feel like we are repeating a pattern that rarely changes, or that there is no perceivable pattern but rather instability or lack of focus. Finding and incorporating a purpose into our lives leads to self-actualization, a feeling that we are fulfilling our unique potential.

Self-Actualization: This Recovery Fundamental is often considered a final stage of development. However, to maintain this stage we must continue to put sufficient and equal amounts of effort into each of the Recovery Fundamentals. Also, a benefit can be found in incorporating the Parallel Recovery Concepts.

Stages of Wellness and Recovery:

Stage one
1- Learning about recovery
2- Exercising choice
3- Seeking services i.e. counseling, therapy, medication, detox, peer support
4- Staying away from harmful behaviors
5- Staying away from negative influences, places or people
6- Ending the pattern of isolation
7- Finding positive role models
8- Learning to ask for support
9- Becoming personally responsible
10- Experiencing joy and distress that can be overwhelming at times (extreme but fickle)

Stage 2
1- Increase in physical health
2- Ability to distinguish between different feelings and handle them
3- Reducing emotions that interfere with our wellbeing
4- Changes in thoughts, feelings and beliefs
5- Zoning in on negative behaviors
6- Having experienced the benefits of recovery, becoming committed to recovery

Stage 4
1- Ability to use our strengths & knowledge to seize opportunities
2- Automatic use of wellness tools and coping skills
3- Self-forgiveness
4- Building loving relationships rather than dependent ones
5- Experiencing enduring happiness

Stage 3
1- Desire to make amends for harm we caused before we began recovery
2- Becoming the "change we want to see in the world"
3- Learning not to inflict self-harm or create hardship
4- Developing honest and trusting relationships with more people

Stage 5
1- Becoming Self-actualized
2- Gaining confidence, gratitude, and acceptance
3- Developing integrity and humility
4- Significant reduction of fear

Stage 6 – Celebration & Maintenance

The Guiding Principles of Recovery
Taken from SAMHSA

Hope – belief that recovery is possible. When Hope is internalized and promoted by others, it is a key driver of recovery.

Person-driven – People define their own goals and the path to reaching them.

Many Pathways/Roads – Recovery is highly personalized and different for each person.

Holistic – Recovery emphasizes mind, body, spirit, and community.

Peer Support – Peers encourage and engage each other.

Relational – Recovery is supported by people who believe in a person's ability to recover.

Culture – Traditions, beliefs, and values are important in defining a person's recovery journey and path.

Trauma-informed – Services should promote safety and trust, creating choice, empowerment, and collaboration.

Strengths & Responsibilities – Individuals, communities, and families have strengths and resources that can benefit recovery. Individuals have the responsibility for their own recovery, but family and community support is essential.

Respect – acceptance and appreciation is key to recovery. This includes respect from other people and a respect for ourselves that helps us develop a positive identity and confidence.

What Mentors should know

- Peer Support is **Self-directed** and works on the principle that clients are the experts on their own experiences and needs. It is a type of therapy based on the idea that each person can become more self-aware, take charge of their own lives, and improve. It is **Person-driven** – People define their own goals and the path to reaching them.

- Peer Support uses **Empathy** a key component of emotional intelligence. **Empathy** is the ability to understand and accurately perceive the internal experiences of another person. In client-centered counseling, Supporters try to show empathy by actively listening to clients, considering their feelings and experiences, and communicating and accepting them.

- In Peer Support, **empowerment** can come from facilitating self discovery and growth by allowing people to to make their own choices and decisions based on their own values, priorities, and goals. The therapist supports the client in identifying their strengths, resources, and areas for growth and assists them in developing coping strategies, problem-solving skills, and self-care practices. **Empathy** also helps counteract **learned helplessness** by creating a safe and supportive environment where clients feel **empowered** to take ownership of their lives and make positive changes.

What Mentors should know

- The **Trauma Informed Approach** demands trust and safety at all levels. This practice encourages choice, collaboration, and empowerment. To practice the Trauma informed approach, request and accommodate feedback as to how to increase the safety of the environment, increase trust by practicing genuineness, and create choice by using open ended and permission questions.

- **Stages of Change** – Stages of change include **Precontemplation, Contemplation, Preparation, Action, and Maintenance**. Often mentors will fail helping someone change behaviors because they do not approach change in the order previously listed. In Precontemplation we educate and develop discrepancy, in Contemplation we encourage and view pros and cons, in Preparation we dismantle barriers, in Action we validate, in Maintenance we should encourage consistency and acquiring more skills related to successful outcomes related to the goal or behavior.

- Some **Cognitive Behavioral Therapy (CBT)** is outside the scope of a Peer Recovery Supporter. Various practices like desensitization techniques and use of imagery are concepts best left to qualified clinicians. However, **relaxation therapy** may be utilized as well as **cognitive behavioral workbooks** that are crafted to address **thoughts, beliefs, and feelings** in a way that does not create excessive pressure on the mentee. Person centered techniques such as building trust and rapport are often helpful but not required as some mentees prefer a more distant expert approach, however this too is outside the scope of a Peer Recovery Supporter.

Differentiate between the medical model and the wellness-focused approach to recovery.

The Medical Model is primarily related to Psychiatry. In the medical model, expert Psychiatrists consider the problems being experienced to be related to genetic inheritance or chemical imbalances. They rely on Medication Assisted Therapy to cause positive change in their patients. This is different from the approach of a Social Worker, Therapist, or Peer Supporter.

A Wellness-focused Approach often involves Peer Support, or the support of someone with lived experience of mental health or substance use; moreover, it considers Social Determinants of Health such as housing, employment, and social support as significant factors of wellbeing.

A Wellness-focused Approach involves **growth, meaning, purpose,** and **empowerment** beyond the problem, which helps a person live the life they want to live.

Day 2

Make sure to prepare for the special exercise found in the section for Self-Care.

Self-Care requires us to make a list of 5 wellness activities we can use to help ourselves feel better. We will discuss our lists of wellness activities in group or in breakout rooms. Please be prepared ahead of time.

Please complete responses to passages and questions included in future groups such as "Day 2" before the next group.

Instructions for passage responses – 1) response must include 3 keywords found in the passage itself. 2) Ensure that the keywords get underlined, so we know which ones you used. 3) the Recovery Concept or Fundamental being linked to the passage must be mentioned twice in the response.

NOTES:

Radical Recovery Peer Support –Liberation Day 2

Insights on Self-Care

Self-care is any healthy action we take to feel better. Sometimes we use Self-Care to respond to stressors, triggering events, or when we feel like we are in crisis. Self-Care that might work normally may not work as well under very difficult conditions.

Tip for dealing with stressors: One suggestion for how to deal with especially difficult situations is to put more time and effort into the things we usually do to make us feel better.

Really good Self-Care is often planned. Planning Self-Care before we feel unwell has benefits, such as, having something to look forward to or helping us not forget Self-Care. Because of this, it is often included in recovery planning.

Examples of Self-Care

- *Remembering our boundaries and what we will or will not do*
- *Being of service to others*
- *Writing a gratitude list*
- *Spending time with family and friends*
- *Getting enough sleep*
- *Taking breaks*

Stressors, burnout, vicarious trauma, poor time management, and compassion fatigue are common reasons we provide Self-Care for ourselves.

- The assignment "how does this passage relate to…?" must include 3 keywords from the passage itself which cannot be used or counted more than once. In addition, the Recovery Concept or Fundamental must be mentioned at least twice in the assignment. <u>Words that do not convey a concept like we, the, or, or a, etc. will not be counted.</u>
- Variations of words that are <u>used in the passages</u> are accepted such as changing "Simple" to "Simplest."
- You must underline the keywords you use.

Self-care

For a long time after getting out of jail, I thought that just taking care of my basic needs like having a place to stay and food to eat was enough. I thought as long as I had those things, I was taking care of myself, but I was missing something important. I realized that focusing only on survival left me feeling empty inside. I had needs for acceptance and feeling like I belonged that weren't being met. That's when bad things would start to happen because I was looking for ways to fill the hole inside.

When I got involved with a recovery program and started working with a mentor, I learned there was more to self-care than just surviving. I learned I needed to take care of my mind and emotions too. Things like learning a new skill or listening to others without trying to make everything about me helped a lot.

Planning for recovery by making goals that weren't just about myself helped me learn more about self-care. Before, I just wanted to focus on things I wanted for myself. But I was told to make goals about helping others too that way I'm not so caught up thinking about myself all the time. It helps me feel more connected and like I have a purpose, which is important when it comes to staying out of trouble.

Example - How Does the Passage connect to Self-Care?

Focusing only on <u>survival</u> left him feeling empty inside. Taking care of his <u>mind and emotions</u> was a form of self-care. Things like learning a new <u>skill or listening</u> to others helped and are common self-care activities.

How Does the Passage connect to Self-Care or Resonate with You?

HOMEWORK

Question - 1:
Am I guilty of not focusing on my survival, emotional, and mental needs? How can I correct this imbalance?

HOMEWORK

Question - 2:
How can I incorporate helping others into my self-care routine?

HOMEWORK

Question - 3:
In what ways can I make goals and plans that not only benefit myself but also benefit those around me?

HOMEWORK

Self-care

I always had a bad habit I could feed into when I was feeling down or if I wanted to have fun, like smoking cigarettes, drinking alcohol, using marijuana or some other drug, or romantic relationships. After some run ins with the law that led to jail time and probation, some people who I was forced to interact with helped me understand that I needed to learn to take care of my whole self - body, mind and spirit.

I began making time each day for small self-care activities like taking a walk or calling a friend just to listen to how they were doing instead of always thinking about myself. These little things helped replace unhealthy habits I relied on in the past and brought me more joy in life.

While overcoming old patterns has been a process, focusing on healthy self-care has been one of the most important tools in my recovery. When I feel urges to return to old behaviors, I try to redirect myself to an activity that improves some part of my life. Continuing to work on whole-person wellness through self-care has kept me on a positive path of growth, eliminated my consumption of alcohol and all drugs besides medically prescribed Marijuana,(since writing this originally, I have stopped smoking medical Marijuana) and helped prevent any further involvement in the criminal justice system.

How Does the Passage connect to Self-Care or Resonate with You?

HOMEWORK

Question - 1:
What are some self-care activities you have found to be helpful in the past?

HOMEWORK

Question - 2:
What are some self-care activities you may have used that you feel were unhelpful or harmful?

HOMEWORK

Question - 3:

Ask someone three things that they do to take care of themselves or make themselves happy and list those three things here.

HOMEWORK

Homework – Provide a List of Wellness Activities

1
2
3
4
5

Recovery Planning

Recovery planning is self-determined but often includes friends and family, supporters, or community leaders. Recovery planning is done with the collaboration of individuals involved and utilizes recovery capital.

A Recovery Plan
- *Is based on self-determination*
- *Identifies strengths of the individual and takes inventory of Recovery Capital*
- *Identifies goals, challenges, action steps, and date of completion*
- *may involve support from others and connection to community resources and leadership.*
- *need to be evaluated and measured for progress. Criteria for evaluation should come from the person creating the plan and should be considered before action, if possible.*

What a Recovery Plan Looks Like on Paper

Goal	Strengths & Recovery Capital	Challenges	Action Steps	Date of Completion
Get Masters Degree	<ul><li>Have a: bachelors degree</li><li>Time: Am on Disability and am self employed</li><li>Experienced with: online courses</li></ul>	Classes are condensed so more is required in a shorter time.	<ul><li>Clear agenda for first week</li><li>Start each day with school first</li><li>Complete all assignments before recreation</li></ul>	August 10th 2025

In the space provided on the extended pages for the recovery Plan, you may also want to include the people who can support you in each goal.

Recovery Planning

When I was in the grips of my addiction, it was causing problems in how I behaved in nearly every aspect of my life, relationships, and work, which led me to regularly get arrested and sent to the county jail. I never took the time to think about what I really wanted out of life or make plans to accomplish goals. In the past my days were all about finding my next fix or buzz without caring too much about how my actions were affecting others or my potential down the road.

Once I entered recovery and started taking it seriously (which took a while), I realized how important it was to plan for my future in a positive way. Early in recovery it was suggested to me that I try developing a recovery plan to work towards. At first this idea didn't interest me much because I felt restricted and oppressed at every turn. However, as described by my sponsor at the time, making a recovery plan isn't just about focusing on myself. They encouraged me to include goals within the community that involved other people. Even though I was limited in what I could do for myself, there were still things I could do to help other people which helped me to avoid isolating and to feel supported.

As I started making some basic plans with the guidance of others, I perceived that I had many more opportunities than I ever knew I had. I just had to pursue them more slowly than people who did not share my burden. No longer was I limited to just getting through each day or satisfying short term desires without regard for consequences. Recovery planning has given me purpose and direction that also helps prevent a return to an old lifestyle that led to ongoing trouble and jail time.

How Does the Passage connect to Recovery Planning or Resonate with You?

HOMEWORK

Question - 1:

Do you struggle making plans for the future ? If so, what is the main reason that is causing the struggle?

HOMEWORK

Question - 2:

What is your reaction to the idea of taking the time to put your plans down on paper in the form of a recovery plan?

HOMEWORK

Question - 3:

How does having an addiction or criminal record impact your ability to plan for the future? Do you believe you can overcome these challenges?

HOMEWORK

Recovery Planning

When I was first sent to jail, I felt like my life was over. All my dreams of having a good job and supporting my family seemed impossible now that I had a criminal record. But at my shelter/rehab, they taught me about recovery planning and how planning was the first step to getting my life back on track.

Struggling is a natural part of recovery when you have a criminal record. Because it's so hard, I still have tough days (increasingly rarer as time goes by) where I'm tempted to go back to my old lifestyle of using drugs or hanging out with people who get me into trouble. Recovery planning has helped me learn how to take care of myself on those hard days.

When I was first arrested, I felt so alone and powerless. But through mentors and support groups, I started to believe that today was the day that I might start to succeed. People in my support network have helped me see that when I'm struggling, I still have choices to make healthy decisions that move me forward. If I want things to get better, I need to make choices each day to work on my recovery.

Now when I make a recovery plan, I think about goals that will help me and help others. Volunteering my time or getting involved in peer support programs gives me purpose and helps other people. I can plan for things that I need to do every day or every so often and I can make plans for the things I really want that will take a lot of effort. Making a plan like this helps me get familiar with what it will take to achieve my goals. Each time I achieve a new goal I become more convinced that I can do other things I never thought I could do before recovery.

How Does the Passage connect to Recovery Planning or Resonate with You?

HOMEWORK

Question - 1:

How does involving others in your recovery planning process make you feel?

HOMEWORK

Question - 2:

How does planning for recovery instead of getting stuck in problems help you take care of yourself on tough days?

HOMEWORK

Question - 3:

In what way does your recovery plan benefit not just yourself but others as well?

HOMEWORK

MENTORING

- Mentoring provides an opportunity to be there for a person in a way that supports them in both the best of times and the worst

- A Mentor utilizes self-disclosure in a way that does not compete with but rather informs an individual of shared experiences

- A good mentor will respect each person's unique approach to recovery

- A Mentor should be primarily focused on the person they are mentoring; only sharing about themselves when it would benefit the mentee

- We never know just what kind of impact we will have on others

- Mentoring is constant and ongoing, and occurs in situations where we present the best or worst aspects of ourselves

What Mentors Should Do

- Identify personal issues that negatively impact one's ability to perform mentor duties and perform appropriate self care before assisting others further.
- Utilize consultation regarding dual relationships.
- Utilize de-escalation techniques and educate individuals on suicide prevention concepts.
- Partner with the individual to access recovery-oriented services and supports
- Support the individual to identify options and participate in decisions connected to creating and completing recovery goals.
- Promote a wellness-focused approach to recovery.
- Utilize supervision and consultation regarding harm to self and others.
- Respond appropriately to personal stressors, triggers and indicators.
- Utilize trauma-informed care approaches.
- Assess the mentee's satisfaction with his/her progress toward recovery goals.

What Mentors Should Do

- Participate as a member of the individual's treatment team.
- Guarantee that recovery is based on the individual's strengths and resiliencies.
- Support the individual in defining spirituality on their own terms.
- Assist others to develop problem-solving skills.
- Assure that relationships, services and supports, reflect individual differences and cultural diversity.
- Support the individual's use of self-determination.
- Model acceptance and cultural humility.
- Partner with individuals to assist them in identifying their strengths, challenges to recovery and recovery capital.
- Apply Motivational Interviewing to assist individuals in during stages of change.
- Inform individuals of their options related to decisions that affect their recovery.

Mahatma Gandhi

- Remember the words of Mahatma Gandhi – **"be the change you want to see in the world."**
- One way to effect change is through Mentoring.

Mentoring

When I was first arrested, all I wanted was to get out of the system and be on my own again. But once I was released, I felt lost and alone. That's when I was introduced to some mentors as part of my criminal diversion court program.

Hearing about the experiences of people who had been where I was and who came out successful really gave me hope. They broke it down for me that even with the restrictions of probation, I still had control over the choices I made each day. If I wanted things to get better, I needed to start making better decisions. My mentors encouraged me to get involved in the recovery community and help others instead of just focusing on myself.

At first it was hard for me to understand how connecting with others could help my reentry into my life, at least when compared to other activities like working a second or third job. But where activities like those could easily leave me feeling burned out, spending time in support groups and volunteering as part of community service could help fill the lonely days that used to lead to using or challenges with my mental health.

I started to realize how much I benefited from the experiences of people further along in their recovery such as insights into jobs that would hire a person with a record. Now I try to mentor anyone just starting out on their recovery journey or who is getting out of jail. I stay closely connected in recovery programs so I can be a positive influence and inspire success in others. Being a mentor has become one of my most important goals, and it helps me stay on the right track too.

How Does the Passage connect to Mentoring or Resonate with You?

HOMEWORK

Question– 1:
Have you ever had a mentor or been a mentor to someone else? How did that experience affect you?

HOMEWORK

Question– 2:

How has connecting with others helped you in difficult times? Can you think of a specific example of when talking to another person has helped you through a difficult time or to improve your life, ifso how did this happen?

HOMEWORK

Question– 3:

What Are a few activities that you believe are a greater priority for you than connecting with other people? It's OK if your answer is that there aren't any activities more important than connecting with other people.

HOMEWORK

Mentoring

Mentoring has played a huge role in my ability to overcome the challenges of having a criminal record. When I was younger, I was constantly told that I wouldn't amount to anything and would end up in jail. Thinking this was the only outcome for me, I had an excuse to give up on my hopes and dreams.

After getting clean and sober and starting on my recovery path I was lucky to find a mentor who believed in me and saw my potential even with my criminal history. Because of this help I was able to create a plan for success, a big part of which involved getting connected with the community to help others and stay accountable for myself. My mentor encouraged me to take on mentees of my own if I believed I could help them.

Sharing my experiences and lessons learned has been incredibly rewarding. It helps me stay on track with my own recovery while giving hope and perspective to others who feel stuck because of their past mistakes. I now have hope that one day my record will be cleared as long as I keep making positive changes. My mentor showed me it's never too late to turn things around and that even people like me, with criminal backgrounds, have so much to offer the world through service, compassion, and leadership. I'm living proof that mentoring can truly transform lives.

How Does the Passage connect to Mentoring or Resonate with You?

HOMEWORK

Question– 1:
how can mentoring others help a person with a criminal record establish a solid reputation in their community?

HOMEWORK

Question– 2:
What do you think the biggest challenge is for a person with a criminal record in providing support to other people?

HOMEWORK

Question– 3:
How do you feel your experiences can benefit others?

HOMEWORK

Mentoring

Having a mentor really helped boost my confidence to believe I could accomplish what I wanted. Their guidance helped me dream bigger. One of the few opportunities that was still available for me was education and part of my newly inspired dreams involved getting an education and developing a skill that would help me better my life. After some minor success with my education in the early years I found that it provided another avenue for me to help others who are struggling.

By accepting the role of being a mentor I could help other people learn the skills that I had learned at school. This helped me practice recovery tools like honesty, trust, and accountability in my life every day. I was also able to spend more time practicing skills learned at school when tutoring others.

One day after I complete my education or have learned even more, I hope to use what I've learned to offer tutoring services professionally as a side job to help other students dealing with challenges. Getting an education helps transform the lives of people when they need it most and being a mentor well help me open the door for others like the door was opened for me.

How Does the Passage connect to Mentoring or Resonate with You?

HOMEWORK

Question– 1:
What personal strengths do you feel you have that could help you help another person? How could using these strengths as a mentor help you further develop your confidence and career goals?

HOMEWORK

Question– 2:

Mentoring requires demonstrating honesty, trust, acceptance, and personal accountability. Which of these characteristics do you feel you are the strongest in and why?

HOMEWORK

Question– 3:

Which of these characteristics do you feel you need the most improvement in and why?

HOMEWORK

The Homework – In the next Year I will

For the current year;

- Create a Recovery Plan Involving 7 goals/activities that you have every day and some activities you will need to do every once in awhile. In the area for the date, if it is not ongoing, list the date of completion; if it is ongoing, state whether it is something that is done every day, or how often it will be done. Please include **both** daily tasks and those we must do every now and then.

- Start with things you struggle with rather than things you find easy.

- Next, create a list of 7 big goals you have, or things that are vitally important that you want to or must do within the year.

- Ensure that this list/Recovery Plan includes how you will support your basic needs like shelter, food and bills. Make the goal specific and attainable.

- During Day 4 we will present a goal from each category of the Recovery Plan and the action steps for the goal.

NOTES:

Radical Recovery Peer Support - Liberation Day 3

Many of us have Baggage. In recovery, we may resist new healthy behaviors and thoughts. This may often stem from a lack of honesty about three factors, 1: that we have been hurt, 2: that we have hurt ourselves or others, and 3: the nature of the severity of the hurt.

It is important to acknowledge

- if we are not honest with ourselves about how we have been hurt, hurt ourselves or others, or the severity, we may repeat unfavorable experiences.

- Lets take a minute to be honest with ourselves about ourselves. On page 150 and 151 you will find a list of virtues, values, and character defects. Please read the directions and complete the activity. Every person has some of each, please indicate at least <u>five</u> of each.

Honesty

In my own experience in early recovery, I lived a life of misleading myself about my own behavior and actions. I pretended as if my actions were the response to something someone else did and that I was only responding to others as they were treating me. I believed everyone was crooked and led by addictions and desires that were harmful to other people or harmful to me.

Even when I entered recovery support groups, I was hesitant to be openly honest about my worst secrets, as that kind of public honesty was new to me. However, I noticed that no one in this environment thought any worse of other people who were being honest and forthcoming about mistakes they had made or how their life was unmanageable. Usually after people share something in a group that would make people outside of the group feel uncomfortable, the sharing was followed by people who said that they could relate to those experiences.

One thing I learned from support groups was that if I was in distress, I should tell somebody about what I was going through so that another person could give me encouragement. Having others witness my progress couldn't be accomplished without other people knowing the truth about where I was starting from, which was an opportunity to be honest that I couldn't have done without, because without witnesses there was no proof of my effort and my progress would seem less real.

How Does the Passage Connect to Honesty or Resonate with You?

HOMEWORK

Question - 1:
How easy or difficult do you find it to be honest with yourself about ways you have been hurt by others or have hurt others through your own actions? What is one experience that has led you to feel this way?

HOMEWORK

Question - 2:

When sharing aspects of your experiences and struggles with others, how do you balance being honest while also feeling comfortable?

HOMEWORK

Question - 3:

Have you ever found yourself blaming others for your own behavior or actions? How has this affected your ability to be honest with yourself and others?

HOMEWORK

Honesty

I once thought that if others did not know about my past then I could pretend that I was like everyone else. That would usually lead to me getting an opportunity I otherwise would have been denied. But as was often the case, when potential employers or other people found out the truth, job offers would be rescinded and opportunities would be lost. Why would I ever want to be honest when the truth usually led to loss?

However, when attending recovery groups, I noticed those who were doing really well were openly sharing even their worst secrets. But no one in the group developed a negative opinion of them; instead, others could relate and said after becoming crimefree for long periods or getting clean and sober, they were able to make amends for past behaviors.

I learned from the people in the group how to share where I was at today and how I was feeling and because of this I received encouragement from them. Being honest about my struggles and temptations invited extra support from others. I realized that by sharing mistakes openly it helps others avoid similar behaviors and setbacks, which is important because I didn't want to see other people go through the same struggles that I went through. Overall, honesty was the key to building trust with myself and finding out that I could trust others as well because I saw firsthand that not everyone would judge me as I always feared.

How Does the Passage Connect to Honesty or Resonate with You?

HOMEWORK

Question - 1:
Have you ever tried to hide a part of your past to avoid negative consequences? How did that work out for you?

HOMEWORK

Question - 2:
Do you think being honest about your struggles and mistakes can help others? Why or why not?

HOMEWORK

Question - 3:

How can being honest about your past help you build trust with yourself and others?

HOMEWORK

Trust

There are different levels of trust:

We can have trust in

- a specific person or people that we trust
- in the systems we are in, such as our governments, legal system, or system of wellness or therapy
- self-trust; <u>trusting that we have our own best interests in mind</u>.

Within these is determining who we can rely on, who we cannot, and what we can share with others.

Tip – (Trust)

❖ **Self-disclosure: It is important to remember**
- we never need to share something that would make us uncomfortable
- there is more we can share with others than something that would make us uncomfortable
- it is different to share things we want to keep private versus our hopes, goals, and stresses
- there is no guarantee what we say will remain confidential

Trust

As a youth, I felt like the system had too much control over me and didn't understand what was really going on in my life. I felt like I had no power and that my dreams for the future didn't matter. When I got older and returned to the system as an adult with a criminal record, I was fearful to repeat my prior experience and didn't trust the authority over me.

Other people in recovery and on probation told me I could have hope again if I was willing to work on my recovery. They told me every day is a chance to change my life for the better. I began to put effort into the things that would give me hope for a better future and I learned that with time and effort anyone can overcome their criminal history if they find support and learn not to put limits on their dreams.

In short, I started to believe that if I was willing to change my behaviors and put in the hard work to better myself each day, then one day things would get better. Now I have reached a point where my record will soon no longer affect me the way it used to. I can pursue more of the goals I have for myself and am helping others through mentor and support programs.

How Does the Passage Connect to Trust or Resonate with You?

HOMEWORK

Question - 1:
Have you ever felt like a system or authority figure had too much control over your life? How did that make you feel about trusting them?

HOMEWORK

Question - 2:
How have your actual experiences with authority figures or systems affected your ability to trust?

HOMEWORK

Question - 3:
Do you trust that with time and effort, anyone can overcome their past and achieve their dreams?

HOMEWORK

Trust

From my perspective, gaining trust was one of the most difficult parts of my recovery journey after getting criminal record. For so long, I believed that I cannot be trusted and therefore no one else could be either. I isolated myself and only associated with others who I thought could help me get what I wanted.

My mentors and sponsor told me that I could build trustworthiness if I could learn to be open and forthcoming with others. Once I found people who didn't abuse my trust, I would have someone to turn to during times I felt like doing something that would be harmful to my life. Over time, gaining the trust of my new support network helped me stay accountable which helped sustain my recovery.

I also came to understand that trust is a two-way street. As I showed myself as reliable through honesty and following through on commitments, it invited trust from others. In return this helped me develop genuine, caring relationships for the first time in my life.

How Does the Passage Connect to Trust or Resonate with You?

HOMEWORK

Question - 1:
Have you ever struggled with gaining someone's trust? How did you handle it, and what did you learn from the experience?

HOMEWORK

Question - 2:
Do you believe that trust is a two-way street, why or why not?

HOMEWORK

Question - 3:
Have you ever lost someone's trust, and had to earn it back? If so, how did you do this?

HOMEWORK

Trust

As someone who has struggled with addiction and been involved in the criminal justice system, it can be difficult to know who you can truly trust for support when you've experienced so much conflict in your life. However, after getting involved in recovery support groups, I found that the people who were most successful in their recovery journeys were willing to trust others, even strangers.

I learned that having at least one safe person you can confide in, like a sponsor or peer supporter, is so important to feeling less alone in the struggle of recovery. When I first started in recovery, I didn't think I could count on or trust others to be there for me. But overtime, by participating with the community and being vulnerable, I've built strong friendships with people who understand what I've been through, and we can support each other through both good and bad times.

While life with mental health and addiction struggles can feel lonely at times, finding people you can trust and connect with is the key to making progress. Forming these types of relationships has helped me feel less defined by my past and gives me hope for the future.

How Does the Passage Connect to Trust or Resonate with You?

HOMEWORK

Question - 1:
How have past experiences of conflict and struggle led you to have difficulty trusting others to offer genuine and helpful support?

HOMEWORK

Question - 2:

In what ways can surrounding yourself with a support network of peers, mentors, and recovery community members help you start building trust in yourself and your ability to succeed?

HOMEWORK

Question - 3:

How can having companionship and someone to trust help support your ongoing recovery journey?

HOMEWORK

Acceptance

Each person is subject to different degrees of unforeseen circumstances, restrictions, rules, and regulations. For the most part, these obstacles depend on our situation, can be temporary, or can be changed with support. While we must deal with these situations while they occur, we can find ways to have hope within them and have Better Days.

*Tip – Trauma/Grief Informed: Many people will report that there are things that they cannot or will not accept. This is okay, remind them that they can still work on other Fundamentals and that there is a difference between 1: accepting that an event took place and 2: accepting an event into our lives and our space.

WE MUST KEEP MOVING

Sometimes, it is the things we find the hardest to accept that take us off the path of our life purpose.

Dr. Martin Luther King Jr. believed that the most important thing each person must do is figure out their life purpose and let nothing hold them back from being the very best at the purpose they have chosen.

While we may struggle to find acceptance, we can let nothing hold us back; in the words of Dr. King **"We must keep moving. If you can't fly, run; if you can't run, walk; if you can't walk, crawl; but by all means keep moving."**

Acceptance

For so long, I struggled to find acceptance because my life up until pursuing recovery had been a catastrophe. Things that happened to me should not happen to anyone. Knowing that I had experienced things that most people do not recover from, I thought about the unfairness of my situation a lot. Where I found that I had little power to make my life the way I wanted it to be, I learned through recovery that time is a great gift. By ending my struggle to accept my past, I found that if I started small, I could begin laying the foundations for a brighter future even if it was a long way off.

As someone who has struggled with trauma, addiction, and been involved in the criminal justice system, and is now in recovery, I understand the importance of acceptance. I learned that I am responsible for my own actions and cannot control everything that happens. Bad things happen to good people.

While the recovery process introduces positive change, it's also true that there will be things out of my control that occur, and people may direct negativity towards me sometimes. Sometimes all any of us can do is continue moving forward, except reality, and complete an honest day's work. The journey isn't easy, but through perseverance and accepting what I can and cannot change, I've been able to achieve some real happiness, where happiness had always been so hard to reach before.

How Does the Passage Connect to Acceptance or Resonate with You?

HOMEWORK

Question - 1:

What are your thoughts on accepting your past, and what steps have you taken to do so?

HOMEWORK

Question - 2:

How can time be a gift when it comes to making up for past mistakes?

HOMEWORK

Question - 3:

How does your experience with addiction or the criminal justice system relate to your understanding of acceptance?

HOMEWORK

Acceptance

Recovery is about continuing to work on yourself even when you're struggling or in pain. For many people who have had experiences similar to mine, we have almost little desire or energy to do this work, and our inability to accept what has happened in the past keeps us from moving forward.

I have learned from participating with other people in recovery that there are always lessons to be learned from hardship and accepting the past, while finding a way to focus on goals for the future. If I continue putting in the effort to better myself, I can develop better thinking and beliefs, which I suspect will improve my quality of life and help me continue to improve. Recovery is a process that isn't always easy, especially when we've been through something really difficult, but through acceptance I've gained hope that things can get better from here.

How Does the Passage Connect to Acceptance or Resonate with You?

HOMEWORK

Question - 1:
Have you been through a difficult experience that you have trouble accepting? How has this affected your ability to work on yourself and move forward?

HOMEWORK

Question - 2:
What are some ways you can practice acceptance in your daily life?

HOMEWORK

Question - 3:
How might practicing acceptance as in question #2 help you in your personal growth and recovery journey?

HOMEWORK

Accepting Your Life – (Page 42)
Original Peer Support Recovery & Coping Skills Workbook and Curriculum

Life happens.

Life will go on whether things have been fair or not.

Life will go on if you have made a big mistake.

Life will go on if you win $1,000,000.

Life will go on no matter what.

Life will go on if you break your arm.

Life will go on if you have surgery.

Life will go on if you have a financial crisis.

I life will go on. Your life will continue.

Accepting Your Life (Continued)

We must accept that life will happen and sometimes there is nothing that we can do about it. If we suffer pain, loneliness, regret, embarrassment or any other difficult feeling, we must accept our life. We must accept our life and we must accept our reality. We must also accept that each and everyone of us has the power within to make a Better Day for ourselves no matter what the circumstances we find ourselves in.

Life will go on no matter what.

I know that I will live my life fighting for that Better Day because I have to.

I have no other option. Better Days are on the way and Better Days are here to stay.

How Does the Passage Connect to Acceptance or Resonate with You?

HOMEWORK

Question - 1:
What are three things that you feel are unfair about your life?

HOMEWORK

1. -

2. -

3. -

Question - 2:
In what three ways do you live your life in a hopeful way?

HOMEWORK

1. -

2. -

3. -

Question - 3:
What are three steps that you could take to make your life better today?

HOMEWORK

1. -

2. -

3. -

Day 4 - Introduction

Please be prepared to discuss a goal for each category of your 6-month Recovery Plan.

Have a great week!

NOTES:

Hope

If we are struggling to find hope, it will often become easier the longer we commit to recovery and with more time between distressing events. Also, we can seek out inspiration by:

- talking to supporters about what is giving our supporters hope

- making lists of things that give us hope

- reading recovery stories

- listing our dreams, and if possible, communicating them to someone

Hope – (Page 4)
Original Peer Support Recovery & Coping Skills Workbook & Curriculum

On Somedays, hope is all I have.

I will fight to live a better life because I want to be happy and successful and because I deserve it.

No one else can tell me that I can't have a better life in which I am happy and healthy.

We decide if we want to live a good and healthy life.

We must reject negative and unhelpful thinking.

Each of us has the power within us to change for the better.

Each of us has a responsibility to work as hard as we can to improve our lives.

We are in control of our lives. Allow yourself to be in control of your life.

We will rise above stigma and be all that we can be.

It will be your victory.

How Does the Passage Connect to Hope or Resonate with You?

HOMEWORK

[ ]

Question - 1:
What are five things that I am proud of in my life?

HOMEWORK

[ ]

HOMEWORK

Question - 2:
What are five things that I most want to improve in my life?

HOMEWORK

Question - 3: Recovery is -?

Hope

Do the mistakes of our past follow us into our future? I once believed that my future was limited because of my past mistakes and that they would always follow me. I had worked so hard to get to a point where I had some control over my ability to create a positive future for myself. But I had all the wrong motivations which were never very positive or socially beneficial. I felt like any bad situation would push me over the edge.

It is true that our criminal records will follow us maybe even for the rest of our lives and some people may never be able to trust us or respect us again. But there is a lot of potential for positive growth and new relationships if we commit to making the next right decision.

I never really was hopeful, not while growing up and not while in my 20s. It took many bumps on the road for me to realize that any hope was good hope. Lacking hope for so long it took a while for me to realize that it was the number one thing people had who were successful. By meeting other successful people, some who didn't have hope for great periods of their own lives, who had found hope and maintained it for years, I learned from their example that no matter what painful things someone goes through, they can still rebuild their life.

It took time to have the same faith as the people I had come to know as my new network of support. My record and past made everything a drag. But over the years, as I focus on my recovery and remain crime free, I notice small improvements happening. In a few years I won't have a criminal record anymore and will be free to benefit from the things I haven't been able to participate in before.

How Does the Passage Connect to Hope or Resonate with You?

HOMEWORK

Question - 1:

Have you ever felt like your past mistakes were holding you back from creating a positive future for yourself, or that you had few opportunities to improve your life? Give an example of one time you've overcome those feelings.

HOMEWORK

Question - 2:

How important do you think hope is for achieving success and why?

HOMEWORK

Question - 3:
Provide an example of a time where someone has dramatically improved their life after a painful experience.

HOMEWORK

Hope

It took a few years of being in recovery for me to get rid of most of my self-doubt, which I had a lot of when I started. Growing up I didn't have many positive role models who believed in me or encouraged me to pursue my dreams and goals. I struggled with this self-doubt and didn't think I was capable of much.

It wasn't until I met a peer supporter during treatment that my perspective on hope began to change. They were one of the first people who genuinely believed I had potential and could accomplish things if I set my mind to it. We had many conversations where they asked me what I wanted for my future and encouraged me to start small with achievable goals.

I slowly realized that by achieving small goals and tasks I could build my skills over time. That gave me hope that one day I could pursue bigger dreams like being consistently employed or getting a college degree. Showing up to work everyday and going back to school seemed impossible when I was deep in my mental health and addiction struggles, but taking it step by step helped hope grow in my heart. I started with getting clean and sober then working on life skills. Each step forward strengthened my belief that I could keep going.

How Does the Passage Connect to Hope or Resonate with You?

HOMEWORK

Question - 1:
How have your past experiences and the people around you influenced your level of self-doubt or lack of self-doubt?

HOMEWORK

Question - 2:

Have you ever had someone in your life who believed in you and encouraged you to pursue your goals? If so, how did that affect your perspective on hope? It's okay if you haven't.

HOMEWORK

Question - 3:

Think about a big dream or goal you have. How can breaking it down into smaller more achievable goals help you succeed? Please provide an example.

HOMEWORK

NOTES:

Personal Responsibility

Some situations may be out of our control or cause discomfort for us. If we are having a hard time fulfilling responsibilities because of obstacles, things outside our control, or things we need or are worried about; we can ask how much control we have over these situations, and if we are doing everything we can within the control we have.

To get back on track we can follow a Recovery Plan that involves:

- A daily plan

- A plan of things we need to do every now and then

- A plan for achieving big goals

Plans should include a way to provide for ourselves and elements of Self-Care.

Personal Responsibility (Continued)

If we are developing a Recovery Plan, it is important to first list things we struggle with, things that need the most attention, or that create new responsibilities for us.

A Recovery Plan is a way to familiarize ourselves with our objectives and requirements and decide how things need to be done.

Personal Responsibility may involve creating goals that improve our lives and our success. For information on how to help someone with their goals, refer to the section of the RRPS Recovery & Mentorship Guide titled Motivational Interviewing & Recovery Planning.

Personal Responsibility

It was easy to blame others for the situation I was in, I truly felt like I had no control over my life or future. Through my recovery process, I began to learn that practicing personal responsibility was one of the most important things I could do to move my life in a positive direction.

Taking responsibility for my actions and their consequences was difficult at first. I had to acknowledge how my past decisions had hurt others and affected my own life. Owning up to that was very freeing. It allowed me to change my focus to the present and future instead of dwelling in regret.

I worked with my sponsor and mentor to develop a recovery plan with goals focused on self-improvement. Things like furthering my education, developing job skills, and getting involved in community service helped me rebuild my sense of purpose and control.

Staying committed to bettering myself one day at a time through that recovery plan gave me a sense of meaning and direction. Reaching small goals along the way motivated me to keep going when times were tough and demonstrated to myself and others that I was serious about change. Overtime, my effort started to outweigh my past mistakes in the eyes of other people.

How Does the Passage Connect to Personal Responsibility or Resonate with You?

HOMEWORK

HOMEWORK

Question - 1:
What usually happens when we blame others for the situation we are in? If you do not do this, think about others who blame things other than themselves for their problems, how does this usually affect them?

Question - 2:
How does owning up to past mistakes help people move forward in a positive direction?

Question - 3:
What specific actions can you take to build your sense of purpose and control?

HOMEWORK

Personal Responsibility

When I decided I wanted to turn my life around, I knew I had to do things different. Part of that was really taking responsibility for myself and my actions. I considered how much I was really doing each day compared to what other people were doing and what I felt like I could manage, and I decided I could definitely start doing more to better myself. College was something easy to get involved in because they had professionals who could help me with every step of the process. The staff at my college were truly there to help me succeed.

At first being so responsible was tough for me. I had to learn to manage my time better and always do my schoolwork. It took me a little while to get used to that, but it wasn't good enough just to pay attention in class, do ok on tests, and miss a homework assignment here and there, I needed to do better than that.

When I first started school there were times where I was so frustrated, I almost gave up, in fact this translated into quite a few missed, or half completed assignments in the beginning. Eventually I got more control over my life while I had been making better decisions for a couple years or more. As I got more control over my life it became easier to manage my assignments and courses.

This can be applied to any area of life, whether in college or not in college, the more responsible we are and the better decisions we make, the more manageable our lives become and the more we can achieve. Now personal responsibility has allowed me to keep up with my life which makes me feel proud. It shows me that even though life was hard before, now I have control over my own future.

How Does the Passage Connect to Personal Responsibility or Resonate with You?

HOMEWORK

Question - 1:
What would your life be like if you took care of all of your responsibilities?

HOMEWORK

Question - 2:
What are some small goals you can set for yourself and how do you think these goals will affect your life?

HOMEWORK

Question - 3:
How might your experience of being frustrated about things interfere with your success?

HOMEWORK

Personal Responsibility

When I was at my rock bottom and struggling the most, I didn't have much motivation to succeed or achieve new opportunities. I had a victim mindset and thought I'd always be a victim. After a few years of focusing on recovery and taking responsibility for myself and my future, I began to grow in so many ways. Being responsible through time management, completing my work on time (and showing up to work), and advocating for myself didn't come easy, but it was worth everything I gave it.

Throughout my years in recovery, these being the more recent years of my life, I have been able to maintain some good jobs which provided for my needs, even though in the many years before this, I felt like I was getting fired every year or two. Today I give every task my all and don't shy away from challenges. When issues come up, I problem solve instead of making excuses.

Today I run my own business and work with many talented professionals. I achieved this with my strong work ethic and dedication. I am still on disability for long term chronic PTSD and bipolar (which helps me supplement my income while I grow my business) but I am taking charge of my life through networking with community leaders and shaping my own destiny with my peer support certification, my bachelor's degree, soon to be master's degree, and being an independent business owner.

Achieving new goals once seemed impossible, but through my recovery and by taking responsibility, my opportunities are endless. I have gained the professional respect of many people and contributed work that others admire. If I keep bettering myself each day and striving to do my best, there's no limit to where I can go. My criminal record has less effect on my life as each day goes by.

How Does the Passage Connect to Personal Responsibility or Resonate with You?

HOMEWORK

Question–1:
Before beginning recovery, how much control did you believe you had over problems and difficulties in your life?

HOMEWORK

Question–2:
How much control do you believe you have today?

HOMEWORK

Question– 3:

Do you have any challenges or shortcomings that can be improved? List 3 and give an example of how you can take accountability for improving the outcome.

HOMEWORK

NOTES:

Self-Advocacy

Sometimes people may feel they have lost their right or ability to advocate for themselves, or that they have lost control of their lives. Each person has the right to advocate for themselves for public benefits and treatment common to their society no matter what the state of their lives.

*Tip — if a person is having a hard time gaining support through self-advocacy, communicate that

- our chances of getting support increase the longer we maintain continued effort with the Recovery Fundamentals that precede this step, especially Personal Responsibility.

- we can believe in ourselves and practice advocating by making a list of goals we think will get the most support and advocating for each item on the list.

What Mentors Should Know

Navigating Services - Mentors will regularly require the services of other professionals to provide support and often make recommendations and referrals for other services. A mentor makes meaningful connections with many local services and leaders. Knowing when to say we don't have all the answers is an important characteristic of a mentor. Finding other providers of services who understand the significance of recovery and wellness versus treatment, and the specific needs for people facing specific challenges is encouraged.

Advocating for Recovery-Oriented Systems involves knowing the organization and leaders of the systems in your area on a deep level. We should develop close relationships with people who might provide recovery services to the people we serve. These deep relationships will inform us if the provider has a recovery-oriented mindset for which to advocate. A Recovery Oriented System of Care is a network of community-based services that meet the total needs of the person in recovery or their families. This includes emotional, occupational, educational, financial, spiritual, physical health, social, and environmental needs.

What Mentors Should Know

- System Level Advocacy – Advocating for changes to rules, policies, or laws that affect how someone lives their lives.

- Self Adovcacy – Because very few people will advocate for us, and because recovery is person-driven, self-advocacy, the process of explaining why you deserve or are qualified for something, is the foundation for a strong recovery.

- Shared decision making – This is the process of a supporter and the person being supported collaborating to develop action plans that are agreed to by both partys.

- Person centered language – Instead of saying "he is an addict", say "name* is a person with an addiction. Instead of saying "they are Bipolar", say "name* is a person diagnosed with Bipolar." Instead of saying "they are a patient", say "name* is a person who is receiving services." Instead of saying "Bro", "Dude", or "Man", say "name*."

Self-Advocacy – (Page 12)
Original Peer Support Recovery & Coping Skills Workbook & Curriculum

Throughout much of my life, I can remember that I have had many times that I needed someone to help me and speak up on my behalf. I had so many needs that were not addressed. Even to this day, I am aware of the extreme damage that has been done to me after years of not having my needs met. As a teenager growing up in many unnatural situations, no one spoke up and advocated for my personal and intimate needs. I was just another troubled teenager living in a group home.

One thing that I wish I learned as many years ago was the act of self-advocacy. After living through some extremely dreadful and horrendous situations, I have learned how to better advocate for myself. Most everything that I have in my life, I have as a result of my self-advocacy.

When we are able to effectively speak up about our needs, then our lives will be better. Self advocacy is our tool - Use it!

How Does the Passage Connect to Self-advocacy or Resonate with You?

HOMEWORK

HOMEWORK

Question – 1:
Give one example of a time you advocated for your needs.

Question – 2:
What is one example where you did not speak up in order to have your needs met and what would you do differently next time?

Question – 3:
What do the words "self-advocacy" mean to you?

HOMEWORK

Self-advocacy

When I entered recovery and started working on myself, the importance of self-advocacy really began to click for me. The whole point of self-advocacy is to get support for things that we can't do by ourselves. This makes sense because some of the best goals that we can make for ourselves are so big that we can't achieve them alone. Before recovery, when I needed something, I didn't say anything because my needs were always ignored or trivialized.

But in my new life of recovery, which really began to feel like living a completely second life compared to the life I had before, I realized that to succeed, I couldn't just hope things would work out on their own, but I needed to take charge of my life and ask for help when I needed it.

After this, when I hit roadblocks on probation like being caught drinking, I explained to my probation officer that my desire to drink got the better of me and now I could use a little assistance. The important point I communicated was that I wasn't drinking because I had a disregard for the rules of my probation, but rather because I just couldn't control my drinking on my own. In this way, I needed support and the only way I could get it was to ask for it. Thinking back on it, I should have asked for help before I got caught because they were so understanding when they found out and got me the help I needed.

How Does the Passage Connect to Self-advocacy or Resonate with You?

HOMEWORK

Question– 1:
How do you usually communicate your needs, strengths, and skills? Give an example of how you have communicated a need, a strength, and a skill.

HOMEWORK

Question– 2:
Do you speak up for your needs when you need something? Why or why not?

HOMEWORK

Question– 3:
Why is self-advocacy important?

HOMEWORK

Self-advocacy

My basic needs were almost always not provided for, but no matter how much I asked or begged for help I was treated without care for my needs. Some people wanted to help me, but others wanted only to hurt me, and it was hard to tell the difference between them. My frustration has led me to scream and shout as ways to get my needs met, but it only makes things worse, especially when I am yelling at the people who are only there to help me.

When I began my recovery from criminal thinking, I started to realize how important self-advocacy is. For so long I felt powerless and like my voice didn't matter. Learning to find the right people to advocate to versus the wrong people and doing the work of speaking up for myself, has allowed me to change my approach when challenges come up. Now, instead of yelling, I explain my situation and ask for understanding and assistance. It's easier to self-advocate for myself and be respected by others when I'm not drinking, high, or yelling.

I realize that I am getting my needs met more today after finding a better way to communicate. Recovery is an everyday process, but I can have more good days when I use my voice to improve my situation and get my needs met in a healthy way.

How Does the Passage Connect to Self-advocacy or Resonate with You?

HOMEWORK

Question–1:
Have you ever felt powerless and like your voice didn't matter? How did you handle that situation?

HOMEWORK

Question–2:
Can you think of a time when you screamed or yelled to get your needs met? How could you have handled this situation differently?

HOMEWORK

Question– 3:
What are some ways you can advocate for yourself right now or within a week at the latest?

HOMEWORK

Day 5 Introduction

- Please be prepared to share one goal from each category of your 1-year Recovery Plan for the next group.

NOTES:

Day 5

Support

"It takes support to fulfill BIG goals. If we do not look for support or accept support from the right people, we will have a tougher time achieving our goals."

If we lack support, developing a strong support system benefits from:

- being mutually supportive to others
- doing everything within our control to maintain our personal definition of wellness
- becoming active in the community, a support group, school or other area like employment
- having several supporters so someone will always be available, and we do not overburden anyone.

Support

When I was actively using drugs and involved in criminal behavior, I was constantly deceiving myself and others about who I really was and what I was doing. I told myself everyone used drugs, everyone broke the law, and everyone argued and broke things, but I was just fooling myself. I had no real sense of identity or purpose other than to feed my addictions and talk a lot of junk.

Once I entered recovery, I started being honest about who I was and the mistakes I had made in the past for the first time. Even though it was scary to open up about things that could make me look bad, I noticed people in the recovery community did not judge each other but instead we're supportive. Through being honest and asking for help, I developed real relationships with others who could relate to my struggles.

As I maintain my recovery and have been honest about my past crimes and challenges staying sober, I feel more secure in who I am and don't hide behind excuses anymore. As my confidence in my identity has grown, I have discovered new strengths and interests. I have found fulfilling roles where I can give back using my lived experience. This helps me feel a sense of purpose and progress.

How Does the Passage Connect to Support or Resonate with You?

HOMEWORK

Question– 1:
Being deceptive can be a barrier to getting support. Have you ever found yourself deceiving others or even yourself about who you really are or what you are doing? Exaggerating something would be a small example of this. How did you feel during this time, and what motivated you to be deceptive?

HOMEWORK

Question – 2:
How have you sought support during times of personal struggle? Please give an example.

HOMEWORK

Question – 3:
What is a time in your life where are you trying to get support but did not get it?

HOMEWORK

Support

It isn't always easy trying to learn new things when you've been through tough times before. I know because I tried it myself. But with the help of others supporting me along the way, I was able to do it. Getting support helped me feel good about myself and stay busy with positive activities instead of doing things that could get me into trouble. Folks at school and in recovery groups asking how I was doing each day really lifted my spirits.

Seeing my peer support person and joining weekly groups with people from my community helped me work on issues from my past too. They took time, listened, and gave advice. Different types of support are out there too like tutoring, counseling, or help finding work. It's smart to ask someone who's been through it for guidance when trying to achieve big goals. Most people like being asked for help in areas of their interest.

Because of my criminal record, I had to be my own biggest supporter sometimes. I talked to the court people about letting me do recovery programs made by people who know what it's like instead of people who learned it from books. Peer groups know what works well because they lived it. More should be done to help systems recognize the value of different paths to recovery.

How Does the Passage Connect to Support or Resonate with You?

HOMEWORK

Question– 1:
Thinking back on times where you did not get the support you needed, how does it make you feel today?

HOMEWORK

Question– 2:
How does being supported or having a lack of support affect your ability to learn and grow?

HOMEWORK

Question– 3:

Think about a time when someone asked you how you were doing, and you felt your spirit's lift. What was it about that interaction that made you feel supported?

HOMEWORK

NOTES:

Purpose

Once we have maintained progress relevant to our interests and security, are more empowered, and have support, we may find that other people are an extension of ourselves or that we have integrated a cause into our lives.

We may also find that
- human rights
- dignity

and
- freedom

become important to us.

Life Blueprint – Purpose
Dr. Martin Luther King Jr.

"You're going to be deciding as the days and the years unfold, what you will do in life, what your life's work will be.

Once you discover what it will be, set out to do it and do it well.

Be a bush if you can't be a tree.

If you can't be a highway, just be a trail.

If you can't be the sun, be a star, for it isn't by size that you win or you fail, be the best of whatever you are."

Purpose

When I first began my recovery journey, I did not have a clear sense of purpose. I struggled to see what meaningful activities or career paths were available to me. However, as I engaged in my education and explored different interests, I started to gain clarity. While in school, I was able to experience various opportunities to help me discover where my passions truly lie.

Although I initially felt my chosen purpose would take a long time to achieve or that I lacked the ability, continuing my education provided hope. I found that my interests changed and evolved over time as I gained new knowledge and experiences. Things that once seemed too complex became clearer as I learned more. Where before I had no interests, now I had many!

Looking back through notes and journals, I was able to see my own personal growth. While I may not have mastered every aspect of my desired field by graduation, I had made significant progress in finding my purpose. My education played a key role in my recovery by providing direction, motivation, and a sense of accomplishment. It has helped me to reclaim something lost from my past and work towards a stable future through a meaningful career. Overall, my purpose continues to drive me forward in both my recovery journey, work, and education.

How Does the Passage Connect to Purpose or Resonate with You?

HOMEWORK

Question–1:

Even if you have very little interest in anything, what is the industry, job, career or field that is the most interesting to you at this point in time? What is something small you can do to find out more information?

HOMEWORK

Question–2:

How might accomplishing smaller instrumental goals help inspire you and boost your self-esteem and confidence as you work towards your longer-term goals?

HOMEWORK

Question– 3:
How can continuing to educate yourself and learning help drive your self discovery process, even if you have not yet found your definitive purpose? (education can be formal or informal)

HOMEWORK

Purpose

For most of my life, all I knew were that there were so many rules telling me "no" when I wanted something, or that the people in my life seem to believe I couldn't do anything or that everything was impossible for me. I didn't have enough money, I didn't have enough education, I didn't know someone who could put me in touch with the right people or network, and I was incredibly socially awkward. In short, whatever it took for other people to achieve their goals, I just didn't have that.

I felt like I'd never call my own shots. Overtime, in different programs, I discovered skills and what work interested me most. Working towards being the person I wanted to be in the end was the only thing that mattered, as long as I could make sure my financial needs and security were provided for. For me, while it was going to take a while to reach some of my other goals, I realized that I had a lot to offer other people who are just starting out with making their lives better. Mentorship is an opportunity to be there for others and may provide income which can help us achieve stability.

Reaching our full potential takes daily small steps. Support networks eased fears that I couldn't make a meaningful difference in my life. We all have gifts, even when life clouds our view. Staying committed to bettering ourselves helps us find our true calling. My criminal history won't define me - my service to others does. YOU have so much to offer too, just trust the process of bettering yourself each day. We can't keep waiting to make changes thinking it will be easier later.

How Does the Passage Connect to Purpose or Resonate with You?

HOMEWORK

Question– 1:
What external factors or obstacles have made you feel like you couldn't pursue your goals in the past?

HOMEWORK

Question– 2:
How have you overcome the obstacles mentioned in question #1, or what steps can you take to overcome them in the future?

HOMEWORK

Question – 3:
When life presents extra stresses, who do you turn to for support to keep you motivated and moving forward?

HOMEWORK

Purpose

I know what it's like to struggle after messing up in the past. It wasn't until I got into recovery that I started to understand important things like finding purpose. Human beings need meaning and purpose to be happy. When we don't have that, it's easy to feel depressed or do things we'll regret later. I felt that way for years - woke up each day with no plans and no drive to better myself.

Recovery taught me that pursuing goals is key. But I had to figure out what really mattered to me first. It took time discovering interests and careers that suited my talents. I started small, scribbling notes each day on what I found interesting. Slowly my skills developed in areas that brought me and others joy and benefit. Even when I picked what gave my life importance, it was difficult believing I could succeed.

I'll tell you; I was in total disbelief a year or two later when I saw how much progress I had made once I committed to pursuing my purpose and dreams and gave them time to become real. Daily improvements and little gains here and there amount to big changes for people who stick with it.

For anyone going through the same things as me, addiction, criminal record, and damaged relationships, don't lose hope. Have faith that your purpose will come, even if it seems far off now. Our paths don't define us - what really counts is who we choose to become next. Making positive impacts helps me stay motivated each morning. I wish that for all folks chasing better days too. Keep your chin up better days are ahead if we work for them.

How Does the Passage Connect to Purpose or Resonate with You?

HOMEWORK

Question– 1:

What do you think it takes to turn your interests into a meaningful career? Give an example of one interest that under the best circumstances and with unlimited resources you think you could turn into a career or business.

HOMEWORK

Question – 2:
What are the support groups, therapies, volunteering experiences, or other activities that you have been involved with that have helped you gain the most perspective on your abilities and interests? Could participating in these areas turn into a purpose for you?

HOMEWORK

Question– 3:
What is one skill or interest that you have become attracted to since you started this program?

HOMEWORK

NOTES:

Self-Actualization

Self-actualization is all about reaching the true potential of our unique selves. Once we have reached our full potential, we may find that we are freer and more capable.

People at this level of development may begin to have a deeper connection with where they believe they fit in the universe, existence, in relation to other people, or with their concept of a higher power.

Self-Actualization (continued)

In the Allegory of the Cave from Plato's *The Republic*, the principal character in the story returns to people who were still "disillusioned" to help them find a better way.

For many, there is a natural inclination by this stage of recovery, to show others a brighter future.

The Parallel Recovery Concept of Mentorship has carried many individuals' recoveries to particularly new heights. Consider the shift in growth demonstrated in the Linear Growth Model due to the Recovery Concept of Mentorship.

Self-actualization

Before 2020, I had never experienced the recovery lifestyle. I didn't know that people could get better or improve their lives. I had seen so many people get stuck in bad situations for long and even longer periods of time. I had so many dreams that had not become reality due to struggles with the criminal justice system from an early age. This was very frustrating for me as a person with a criminal record trying to reach my true potential.

Having a criminal record made it very difficult to pursue opportunities and feel a sense of purpose, which are an important part of self-actualization. Not to mention, having a criminal record was embarrassing. However, once I learned that people could change their destiny, I started to realize that with hard work and dedication to bettering myself, my situation did not have to define me forever. I needed to consider that my dreams and goals were possibilities that I could make progress toward.

Even though progress was slow at first, I continued to work on myself and develop my skills and capabilities in spite of previous disappointments. I am making progress. Gradually, as I gained more experience and put my effort into responsibilities like work, school, mending broken relationships, and recovery, my confidence and self-esteem grew. I started to see a future where I could overcome the limitations of my past and achieve a happier, more fulfilling life as a member of my community.

How Does the Passage Connect to Self-Actualization or Resonate with You?

HOMEWORK

HOMEWORK

Question– 1:
Think of one challenge you're facing on the road to becoming the person you want to be. Please write down what that challenge is and answer how you will overcome that challenge.

Question– 2:
How would your perspective or goals change if you knew for absolute certainty that people can purposely change their destiny?

Question – 3:

In what ways has your confidence, self-esteem, and belief in your ability to become the person you want to be, grown since you started this program?

HOMEWORK

Self-actualization

Looking back on my interactions with the criminal justice system, I can see how constantly fighting my situation, the rules, and authority was using up the time I could be spending on improving my life. It truly didn't matter how unhappy I was with being on probation and the rules I had to follow, my legal situation was only temporary, and I had work to do to improve my life.

Being in the criminal system and facing so many restrictions and rules, I felt very confined and limited. It was difficult to imagine achieving my full potential under the control of others. As I engaged in recovery work and started accomplishing small goals, I started to imagine bigger dreams for myself. I discovered talents and interests I never knew I had.

A key realization for me was that self-actualization could only be achieved by myself, this is why it's called "self" actualization, Because the only person who can achieve my full potential is me. No external forces or limitations could define my capabilities unless I allowed it. I could achieve anything that anyone else could achieve if I was willing to do the work.

While the legal systems rules were hard to get used to because of the habits and behaviors I had for so long, I recognized they were ultimately part of the process of improving my life. My habits and behaviors were not good for me and probably have already taken 20 years from my life, time I'll never get back. Learning to stay determined to fulfill my unique purpose no matter what my situation, has helped me overcome barriers and challenges related to my criminal history.

How Does the Passage Connect to Self-Actualization or Resonate with You?

HOMEWORK

Question – 1:
Do you constantly fight your situation, the rules, and authority? If so, how does this affect the time you have to work on other areas of your life? It's okay if you don't do this.

HOMEWORK

Question– 2:
How can you overcome feeling confined and limited by external forces, such as the criminal justice system, to achieve your full potential?

HOMEWORK

Question– 3:
What habits and behaviors do you have that are slowing your progress?

HOMEWORK

Recap & Conclusion

This curriculum emphasizes balanced linear growth through the development of 9 Recovery Fundamentals and three Parallel Recovery Concepts that occur alongside each of the 9 Fundamentals.

 **The goals of this program are based on the Fundamentals of Recovery and the Recovery Concepts and are to teach participants how to:**

 Learn to develop a Recovery Plan to take recovery to greater heights (Recovery Planning)

 Learn the importance of and how to perform Self-Care

 overcome challenges or troubling thoughts, handle stressful or difficult situations, achieve personal growth and wellness, and live a self-directed life

 learn that while participating in recovery we are at every moment a mentor and a model of recovery behavior

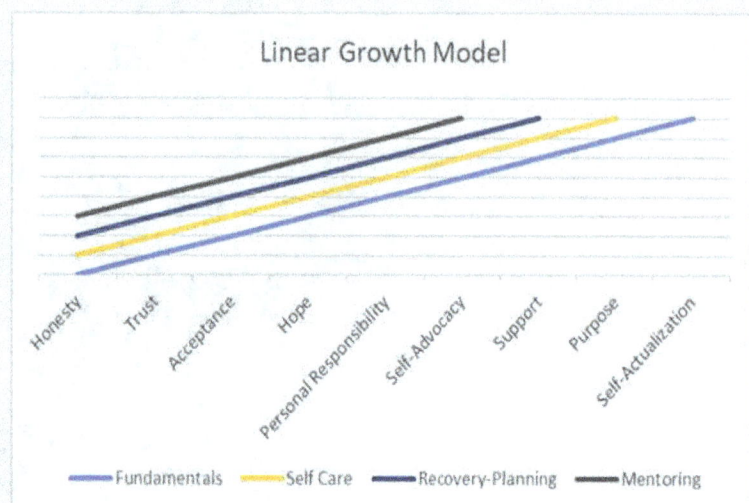

The Linear Growth Model

The Linear Growth Model gets its name from the idea that

- Growth is usually Non-Linear
- we want to put consistent effort into each of the 9 Fundamentals which will result in more, but not all, consistent experiences in our lives.
- When developed inconsistently with this format, inconsistent and unexpected outcomes may occur.
- When developed in the order listed previously, each of the 9 Recovery Fundamentals assists in the cultivation and growth of the other Fundamentals.
- When Utilizing the Parallel Recovery Concepts in conjunction with the Recovery Fundamentals, we can shift our results to a better outcome

Mahatma Gandhi, the great Indian spiritual leader, said, "Be the change you want to see in the world."

From the Better Days workbook passage 'Creating Change': "I say that first I must change myself into the person I want to be."

The words from the passage 'Creating Change' and Mahatma Gandhi indicate that by learning to focus on our personal experience of growth and change in the direction of our own interest, the world, will change in our direction, as we model the behaviors we want to see in the world.

Many programs say that giving back and helping others with the same problems as we have experienced is a sort of final step. Many people who have been successful in Recovery say that **giving back, taking commitments to support others,** and **remembering that they are an example of recovery in their communities** helped them the most in their recovery.

The reasoning of this program and in Peer Support in general is that showing recovery is possible occurs alongside every stage in the process and our actions create a lasting impact.

Stages of Wellness and Recovery:

Stage one
1- Learning about recovery
2- Exercising choice
3- Seeking services i.e. counseling, therapy, medication, detox, peer support
4- Staying away from harmful behaviors
5- Staying away from negative influences, places or people
6- Ending the pattern of isolation
7- Finding positive role models
8- Learning to ask for support
9- Becoming personally responsible
10- Experiencing joy and distress that can be overwhelming at times (extreme but fickle)

Stage 2
1- Increase in physical health
2- Ability to distinguish between different feelings and handle them
3- Reducing emotions that interfere with our wellbeing
4- Changes in thoughts, feelings and beliefs
5- Zoning in on negative behaviors
6- Having experienced the benefits of recovery, becoming committed to recovery

Stage 3
1 - Desire to make amends for harm we caused before we began recovery
2 - Becoming the "change we want to see in the world"
3 - Learning not to inflict self-harm or create hardship
4 - Developing honest and trusting relationships with more people

Stage 4
1 - Ability to use our strengths & knowledge to seize opportunities
2 - Automatic use of wellness tools and coping skills
3 - Self-forgiveness
4 - Building loving relationships rather than dependent ones
5 - Experiencing enduring happiness

Stage 5
1 - Becoming Self-actualized
2 - Gaining confidence, gratitude, and acceptance
3 - Developing integrity and humility
4 - Significant reduction of fear

Stage 6 - Celebration & Maintenance

The 10 Guiding Principles of Recovery

Taken From SAMHSA

Hope – belief that recovery is possible. When Hope is internalized and promoted by others, it is a key driver of recovery.

Person-driven – People define their own goals and the path to reaching them. Noone achieves them for us.

Many Pathways/Roads – Recovery is highly personalized and different for each person.

Holistic – Recovery emphasizes mind, body, spirit, and community.

Peer Support – Peers encourage and engage each other.

Relational – Recovery is supported by people who believe in a person's ability to recover.

Culture – Traditions, beliefs, and values are important in defining a person's recovery journey and path.

Trauma-informed – Support should promote safety and trust, creating choice, empowerment, and collaboration.

Strengths & Responsibilities – Individuals, communities, and families have strengths and resources that can benefit recovery. Individuals have the responsibility for their own recovery, but family and community support are essential.

Respect – acceptance and appreciation are key to recovery. This includes respect from other people and a respect for ourselves that help us develop a positive identity and confidence.

What Mentors Should Do

- Identify personal issues that negatively impact one's ability to perform mentor duties and perform appropriate self care before assisting others further.
- Utilize consultation regarding dual relationships.
- Utilize de-escalation techniques and educate individuals on suicide prevention concepts.
- Partner with the individual to access recovery-oriented services and supports
- Support the individual to identify options and participate in decisions connected to creating and completing recovery goals.
- Promote a wellness-focused approach to recovery.
- Utilize supervision and consultation regarding harm to self and others.
- Respond appropriately to personal stressors, triggers and indicators.
- Utilize trauma-informed care approaches.
- Assess the mentee's satisfaction with his/her progress toward recovery goals.

What Mentors Should Do

- Participate as a member of the individual's treatment team.
- Guarantee that recovery is based on the individual's strengths and resiliencies.
- Support the individual in defining spirituality on their own terms.
- Assist others to develop problem-solving skills.
- Assure that relationships, services and supports, reflect individual differences and cultural diversity.
- Support the individual's use of self-determination.
- Model acceptance and cultural humility.
- Partner with individuals to assist them in identifying their strengths, challenges to recovery and recovery capital.
- Apply Motivational Interviewing to assist individuals in during stages of change.
- Inform individuals of their options related to decisions that affect their recovery.

What Mentors Should Know

- System Level Advocacy – Advocating for changes to rules, policies, or laws that affect how someone lives their lives.
- Self Adovcacy – Because very few people will advocate for us, and because recovery is person-driven, self-advocacy, the process of explaining why you deserve or are qualified for something, is the foundation for a strong recovery.
- Shared decision making – This is the process of a supporter and the person being supported collaborating to develop action plans that are agreed to by both partys.
- Person centered language – Instead of saying "he is an addict", say "name* is a person with an addiction. Instead of saying "they are Bipolar", say "name* is a person diagnosed with Bipolar." Instead of saying "they are a patient", say "name* is a person who is receiving services." Instead of saying "Bro", "Dude", or "Man", say "name*."

What Mentors Should Know

Navigating Services - Mentors will regularly require the services of other professionals to provide support and often make recommendations and referrals for other services. A mentor makes meaningful connections with many local services and leaders. Knowing when to say we don't have all the answers is an important characteristic of a mentor. Finding other providers of services who understand the significance of recovery and wellness versus treatment, and the specific needs for people facing specific challenges is encouraged.

Advocating for Recovery-Oriented Systems involves knowing the organization and leaders of the systems in your area on a deep level. We should develop close relationships with people who might provide recovery services to the people we serve. These deep relationships will inform us if the provider has a recovery-oriented mindset for which to advocate. A Recovery Oriented System of Care is a network of community-based services that meet the total needs of the person in recovery or their families. This includes emotional, occupational, educational, financial, spiritual, physical health, social, and environmental needs.

NOTES:

VIRTUES & VALUES

Please circle each value you feel describes who you are. Reflect on if you hold these values in high regard and what it means to you to posses this value. Consider if the values you didn't circle are important to you and determine what it would look like for you to posses that value and how you can incorporate it into your lifestyle. <u>Try to be as honest with yourself as you can during this exercise.</u> This is not an extensive list.

Orderliness	Generosity	Courage	Wisdom
Justice	Self-control	Assertiveness	Helpfulness
Modesty	Peacefulness	Service	Forgiveness
Purposefulness	Good Counsel	Responsibility	
Kindness	Honesty	Respect	Tolerance
Perseverance	Good judgment	Gratitude	Humility
Obedience	Patience	Leadership/Command	
Truthfulness	Moderation	Loyalty	Courtesy
Friendliness	Sincerity	Prayerfulness	
Greatness/Magnanimity		Docility	Industriousness
Foresight	Patriotism		
Meekness	Tact		

CHARACTER DEFECTS

Please circle each character defect you feel describes who you are. Reflect on your thoughts about the defects you circled. Determine if you would like to make a change to improve in these areas. <u>Try to be as honest with yourself as you can during this exercise.</u> This is not an extensive list.

Resentment	Cowardice	Self-Pity
Self-Justification	Self-Importance	Self-Condemnation
Lying and Evasiveness	Impatience	Hate
False Pride	Jealousy	Envy
Laziness	Procrastination	Insincerity
Negative Thinking	Immoral Thinking	Perfectionism
Criticizing	Greed	Distrustfulness
Hypochondria	Being Thin-Skinned	Moodiness
Being a Buzzkill	Willful Ignorance	callousness
Cruelty	Violence	Rigidity
Diffidence	Lechery	Self-Indulgence
Being a Know-It-All	Naiveté	Immaturity
Fastidiousness	Being overly picky	Prejudice
Rudeness	Crassness	

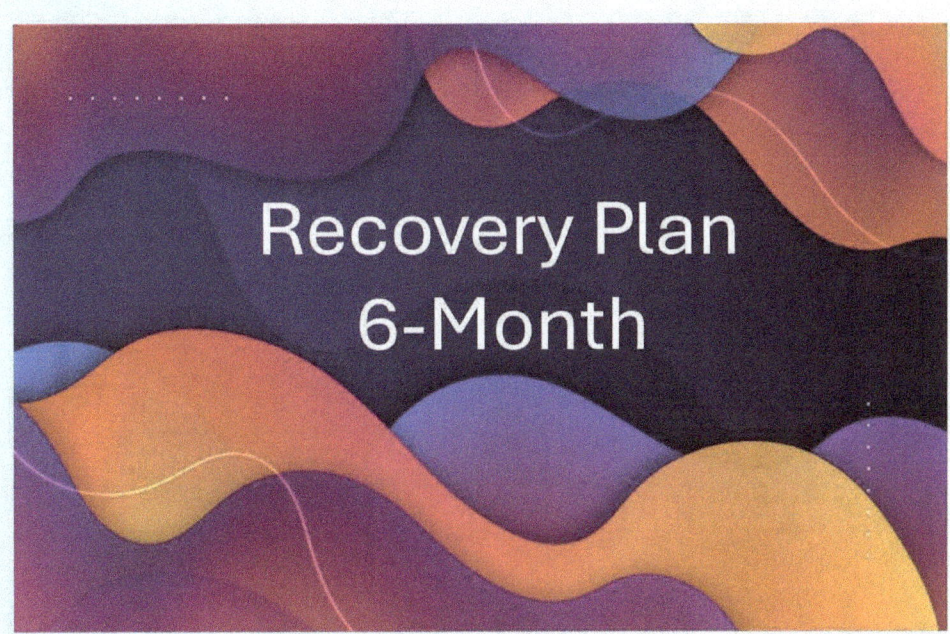

Note: You can use the pages with lines to add extra action steps that can't be fit into the colored tables.

"What I do in the 168 hours of the week."

Be as specific as possible, have at least 1 activity for every line, you can do multiple activities at the same time.

_____

_____

_____

_____

_____

_____

_____

_____

_____

_____

_____

_____

6 Month – Everyday Goals

Goal #1 _____

_____

Strengths & Recovery Capital	Challenges	Action Steps	Date of Completion

Goal #1
Goal Description
_____

Action Steps

- _____

  _____

- _____

  _____

- _____

  _____

- _____

  _____

- _____

  _____

- People

  Involved_____

  _____

- _____

  _____

6 Month – Everyday Goals

Goal #2 _____

_____

Strengths & Recovery Capital	Challenges	Action Steps	Date of Completion

Goal #2
Goal Description
_____

Action Steps

- _____
  _____

- _____
  _____

- _____
  _____

- _____
  _____

- _____
  _____

- People

  Involved_____

  _____

- _____
  _____

6 Month– Everyday Goals

Goal #3 _____

_____

Strengths & Recovery Capital	Challenges	Action Steps	Date of Completion

Goal #3
Goal Description
_____

Action Steps

- _____

  _____

- _____

  _____

- _____

  _____

- _____

  _____

- _____

  _____

- People

  Involved_____

  _____

- _____

  _____

6 Month– Everyday Goals

Goal #4 _____

_____

Strengths & Recovery Capital	Challenges	Action Steps	Date of Completion

Goal #4
Goal Description
_____

Action Steps

- _____
  _____
  _____

- _____
  _____
  _____

- _____
  _____
  _____

- _____
  _____
  _____

- _____
  _____

- People
  Involved_____
  _____

- _____
  _____

6 Month– Goals We Need Once in a While

Goal #5 _____

_____

Strengths & Recovery Capital	Challenges	Action Steps	Date of Completion

Goal #5
Goal Description
_____

Action Steps

- _____

  _____

- _____

  _____

- _____

  _____

- _____

  _____

- _____

  _____

- People

  Involved_____

  _____

- _____

  _____

6 Month – Goals We Need Once in a While

Goal #6 _____

_____

Strengths & Recovery Capital	Challenges	Action Steps	Date of Completion

Goal #6
Goal Description
_____

Action Steps

- _____

   _____

- _____

   _____

- _____

   _____

- _____

   _____

- _____

   _____

- People

   Involved_____

   _____

- _____

   _____

6 Month – Goals We Need Once in a While

Goal #7 _____

_____

Strengths & Recovery Capital	Challenges	Action Steps	Date of Completion

Goal #7
Goal Description
_____

Action Steps

- _____

    _____

- _____

    _____

- _____

    _____

- _____

    _____

- _____

    _____

- People

    Involved_____

    _____

- _____

    _____

6 Month – Big Achievements

Goal #8 _____

_____

Strengths & Recovery Capital	Challenges	Action Steps	Date of Completion

Goal #8
Goal Description
_____

Action Steps

- _____
  _____

- _____
  _____

- _____
  _____

- _____
  _____

- _____
  _____

- People
  Involved_____
  _____

- _____
  _____

6 Month – Big Achievements

Goal #9 _____

_____

Strengths & Recovery Capital	Challenges	Action Steps	Date of Completion

Goal #9
Goal Description
_____

Action Steps

- _____

  _____

- _____

  _____

  _____

- _____

  _____

  _____

- _____

  _____

  _____

- _____

  _____

- People

  Involved_____

  _____

- _____

  _____

6 Month – Big Achievements

Goal #10

_____

_____

Strengths & Recovery Capital	Challenges	Action Steps	Date of Completion

Goal #10
Goal Description
_____

Action Steps

- _____

  _____

  _____

- _____

  _____

  _____

- _____

  _____

  _____

- _____

  _____

  _____

- _____

  _____

- People

  Involved_____

  _____

- _____

  _____

6 Month – Big Achievements

Goal #11
_____

_____

Strengths & Recovery Capital	Challenges	Action Steps	Date of Completion

Goal #11
Goal Description
_____

Action Steps

- _____

  _____

- _____

  _____

  _____

- _____

  _____

  _____

- _____

  _____

  _____

- _____

  _____

- People

  Involved_____

  _____

- _____

  _____

6 Month – Big Achievements

Goal #12
_____

_____

Strengths & Recovery Capital	Challenges	Action Steps	Date of Completion

Goal #12
Goal Description
_____

Action Steps

- _____
  _____

- _____
  _____

- _____
  _____

- _____
  _____

- _____
  _____

- People

  Involved_____

  _____

- _____
  _____

6 Month – Big Achievements

Goal #13

_____

_____

Strengths & Recovery Capital	Challenges	Action Steps	Date of Completion

Goal #13
Goal Description
_____

Action Steps

- _____

 _____

- _____

 _____

- _____

 _____

- _____

 _____

- _____

 _____

- People

 Involved_____

 _____

- _____

 _____

6 Month – Big Achievements

Goal #14

_____

_____

Strengths & Recovery Capital	Challenges	Action Steps	Date of Completion

Goal #14
Goal Description
_____

Action Steps

- _____

  _____

- _____

  _____

  _____

- _____

  _____

  _____

- _____

  _____

  _____

- _____

  _____

- People

  Involved_____

  _____

- _____

  _____

Year 1 – Everyday Goals

Goal #1 _____

_____

Strengths & Recovery Capital	Obstacles	Action Steps	Date of Completion

Goal #1
Goal Description
_____

Action Steps

- _____

  _____

- _____

  _____

  _____

- _____

  _____

- _____

  _____

- _____

  _____

- People

  Involved_____

  _____

- _____

  _____

Year 1 – Everyday Goals

Goal #2 _____

_____

Strengths & Recovery Capital	Obstacles	Action Steps	Date of Completion

Goal #2
Goal Description
_____

Action Steps

- _____
  _____

- _____
  _____
  _____

- _____
  _____
  _____

- _____
  _____
  _____

- _____
  _____

- People

  Involved_____
  _____

- _____
  _____

Year 1 – Everyday Goals

Goal #3 _____

_____

Strengths & Recovery Capital	Obstacles	Action Steps	Date of Completion

Goal #3
Goal Description
_____

Action Steps

- _____

  _____

- _____

  _____

- _____

  _____

- _____

  _____

- _____

  _____

- People

  Involved_____

  _____

- _____

  _____

Year 1 – Everyday Goals

Goal #4 _____

_____

Strengths & Recovery Capital	Obstacles	Action Steps	Date of Completion

Goal #4
Goal Description
_____

Action Steps

- _____
  _____

- _____
  _____
  _____

- _____
  _____
  _____

- _____
  _____
  _____

- _____
  _____

- People Involved_____
  _____

- _____
  _____

Year 1 – Goals We Need Once in a While

Goal #5 _____

_____

Strengths & Recovery Capital	Obstacles	Action Steps	Date of Completion

Goal #5
Goal Description
_____

Action Steps

- _____
  _____

- _____
  _____
  _____

- _____
  _____

- _____
  _____

- _____
  _____

- People Involved_____
  _____

- _____
  _____

Year 1 – Goals We Need Once in a While

Goal #6 _____

_____

Strengths & Recovery Capital	Obstacles	Action Steps	Date of Completion

Goal #6
Goal Description
_____

Action Steps

- _____
  _____
  _____

- _____
  _____
  _____

- _____
  _____
  _____

- _____
  _____
  _____

- _____
  _____
  _____

- People
  Involved_____
  _____

- _____
  _____

Year 1 – Goals We Need Once in a While

Goal #7 _____

_____

Strengths & Recovery Capital	Obstacles	Action Steps	Date of Completion

Goal #7
Goal Description
_____

Action Steps

- _____
  _____

- _____
  _____

- _____
  _____

- _____
  _____

- _____
  _____

- People Involved_____
  _____

- _____
  _____

Year 1 – Big Achievements

Goal #8 _____

_____

Strengths & Recovery Capital	Obstacles	Action Steps	Date of Completion

Goal #8
Goal Description
_____

Action Steps

- _____
  _____

- _____
  _____
  _____

- _____
  _____
  _____

- _____
  _____
  _____

- _____
  _____

- People
  Involved_____
  _____

- _____
  _____

Year 1 – Big Achievements

Goal #9 _____

_____

Strengths & Recovery Capital	Obstacles	Action Steps	Date of Completion

Goal #9
Goal Description
_____

Action Steps

- _____

  _____

- _____

  _____

  _____

- _____

  _____

- _____

  _____

- _____

  _____

- People

  Involved_____

  _____

- _____

  _____

Year 1 – Big Achievements

Goal #10

_____

_____

Strengths & Recovery Capital	Obstacles	Action Steps	Date of Completion

Goal #10
Goal Description
_____

Action Steps

- _____
  _____

- _____
  _____
  _____

- _____
  _____
  _____

- _____
  _____
  _____

- _____
  _____

- People Involved_____
  _____

- _____
  _____

Year 1 – Big Achievements

Goal #11

_____

_____

Strengths & Recovery Capital	Obstacles	Action Steps	Date of Completion

Goal #11
Goal Description
_____

Action Steps

- _____
  _____
  _____

- _____
  _____
  _____
  _____

- _____
  _____
  _____

- _____
  _____
  _____

- _____
  _____

- People

  Involved_____
  _____

- _____
  _____

Year 1 – Big Achievements

Goal #12
_____

_____

Strengths & Recovery Capital	Obstacles	Action Steps	Date of Completion

Goal #12
Goal Description
_____

Action Steps

- _____

    _____

- _____

    _____

    _____

- _____

    _____

    _____

- _____

    _____

    _____

- _____

    _____

- People Involved_____

    _____

- _____

    _____

Year 1 – Big Achievements

Goal #13
_____

_____

Strengths & Recovery Capital	Obstacles	Action Steps	Date of Completion

Goal #13
Goal Description
_____

Action Steps

- _____

  _____

- _____

  _____

- _____

  _____

- _____

  _____

- _____

  _____

- People

  Involved_____

  _____

- _____

  _____

Year 1 – Big Achievements

Goal #14

_____

_____

Strengths & Recovery Capital	Obstacles	Action Steps	Date of Completion

Goal #14
Goal Description
_____

Action Steps

- _____

  _____

- _____

  _____

- _____

  _____

- _____

  _____

- _____

  _____

- People

  Involved_____

  _____

- _____

  _____

3 year – Everyday Goals

Goal #1 _____

_____

Strengths & Recovery Capital	Obstacles	Action Steps	Date of Completion

Goal #1
Goal Description
_____

Action Steps

- _____

  _____

- _____

  _____

- _____

  _____

- _____

  _____

- _____

  _____

- People

  Involved_____

  _____

- _____

  _____

3 year– Everyday Goals

Goal #2 _____

_____

Strengths & Recovery Capital	Obstacles	Action Steps	Date of Completion

Goal #2
Goal Description
_____

Action Steps

- _____

  _____

- _____

  _____

- _____

  _____

- _____

  _____

- _____

  _____

- People

  Involved_____

  _____

- _____

  _____

3 year– Everyday Goals

Goal #3 _____

_____

Strengths & Recovery Capital	Obstacles	Action Steps	Date of Completion

Goal #3
Goal Description
_____

Action Steps

- _____

  _____

- _____

  _____

- _____

  _____

- _____

  _____

- _____

  _____

- People

  Involved_____

  _____

- _____

  _____

3 year– Everyday Goals

Goal #4 _____

_____

Strengths & Recovery Capital	Obstacles	Action Steps	Date of Completion

Goal #4
Goal Description
_____

Action Steps

- _____

  _____

- _____

  _____

- _____

  _____

- _____

  _____

- _____

  _____

- People

  Involved_____

  _____

- _____

  _____

3 year– Goals We Need Once in a While

Goal #5 _____

_____

Strengths & Recovery Capital	Obstacles	Action Steps	Date of Completion

Goal #5
Goal Description
_____

Action Steps

- _____

  _____

- _____

  _____

- _____

  _____

- _____

  _____

- _____

  _____

- People

  Involved_____

  _____

- _____

  _____

3 year– Goals We Need Once in a While

Goal #6 _____

_____

Strengths & Recovery Capital	Obstacles	Action Steps	Date of Completion

Goal #6
Goal Description
_____

Action Steps

- _____

  _____

- _____

  _____

- _____

  _____

- _____

  _____

- _____

  _____

- People

  Involved_____

  _____

- _____

  _____

3 year– Goals We Need Once in a While

Goal #7 _____

_____

Strengths & Recovery Capital	Obstacles	Action Steps	Date of Completion

Goal #7
Goal Description
_____

Action Steps

- _____
  _____

- _____
  _____

- _____
  _____

- _____
  _____

- _____
  _____

- People

  Involved_____
  _____

- _____
  _____

3 year– Big Achievements

Goal #8 _____

_____

Strengths & Recovery Capital	Obstacles	Action Steps	Date of Completion

Goal #8
Goal Description
_____

Action Steps

- _____
  _____

- _____
  _____

- _____
  _____

- _____
  _____

- _____
  _____

- People

  Involved_____

  _____

- _____
  _____

3 year – Big Achievements

Goal #9 _____

_____

Strengths & Recovery Capital	Obstacles	Action Steps	Date of Completion

Goal #9
Goal Description
_____

Action Steps

- _____
  _____

- _____
  _____

- _____
  _____

- _____
  _____

- _____
  _____

- People
  Involved_____
  _____

- _____
  _____

3 year– Big Achievements

Goal #10

_____

_____

Strengths & Recovery Capital	Obstacles	Action Steps	Date of Completion

Goal #10
Goal Description
_____

Action Steps

- _____
  _____

- _____
  _____

- _____
  _____

- _____
  _____

- _____
  _____

- People

  Involved_____
  _____

- _____
  _____

3 year – Big Achievements

Goal #11
_____

_____

Strengths & Recovery Capital	Obstacles	Action Steps	Date of Completion

Goal #11
Goal Description
_____

Action Steps

- _____

  _____

- _____

  _____

- _____

  _____

- _____

  _____

- _____

  _____

- People

  Involved_____

  _____

- _____

  _____

3 year – Big Achievements

Goal #12
_____

_____

Strengths & Recovery Capital	Obstacles	Action Steps	Date of Completion

Goal #12
Goal Description
_____

Action Steps

- _____
  _____

- _____
  _____
  _____

- _____
  _____
  _____

- _____
  _____
  _____

- _____
  _____

- People

  Involved_____
  _____

- _____
  _____

3 year– Big Achievements

Goal #13

_____

_____

Strengths & Recovery Capital	Obstacles	Action Steps	Date of Completion

Goal #13
Goal Description
_____

Action Steps

- _____

  _____

- _____

  _____

- _____

  _____

- _____

  _____

- _____

  _____

- People

  Involved_____

  _____

- _____

  _____

3 year– Big Achievements

Goal #14

_____

_____

Strengths & Recovery Capital	Obstacles	Action Steps	Date of Completion

Goal #14
Goal Description
_____

Action Steps

- _____

  _____

  _____

- _____

  _____

  _____

- _____

  _____

  _____

- _____

  _____

  _____

- _____

  _____

- People

  Involved_____

  _____

- _____

  _____

Facilitation Process

Level 1 Groups – Co-facilitator Required*

The slides that can be read in the workbook or PowerPoint will be divided between all those wishing to receive a certificate of participation or completion, including participation from the facilitators. The Facilitators will start by explaining why we request full participation and the reward of either a certificate of completion or participation. The Information on participation requirements is on page two underneath the table of contents.

The Facilitators will read the first two slides of the first presentation. After that, all slides will be divided up between the participants. The exceptions to this are the slides in the first session's presentation following the slide title "Why We Present the Recovery Fundamentals and Parallel Recovery Concepts in this Order." These slides sometimes contain more than one Fundamental or Concept and there will be a different reader for each of these.

At the end of each session, the Facilitator will read the last slide that conveys information related to the upcoming session. After this, the remainder of the time will be spent on open discussion of the day's session. For session one this will be the full span of 2 hours, for the remaining session it will be the span of 3 hours.

The remaining sessions also have sections titled 'How does this passage connect or relate to the concept or fundamental.' These questions entail a short response that should connect the passage read just before this question to the Recovery Concept or Fundamental being discussed at the time. Everyone has the capability to answer these questions so everyone desiring a certificate of participation or completion will answer these including the facilitator, unless facilitator participation means some participants will not have the chance to participate.

Participation points will not be lost for these questions if there were not enough questions for everyone to get a chance to participate. A participation sheet will be provided which specifies how many participation points a person will need in each category of participation. For those who have not had a chance to answer these questions, they will have an opportunity to revisit them at the end of the group.

Sessions 2 – 5 also have many short questions. There are usually 3 questions for each passage. These are divided between all those seeking a certificate of completion and the Facilitators. These questions are not required to be answered by those seeking a certificate of participation.

The Facilitator will not participate or read unless there are fewer than 5 people attempting a certificate of completion, in which case, only participating when they have the least amount of participation compared to those seeking a certificate. Participants can choose when they would like to participate in order to get the right amount of participation points, however when some of them are close to full points, the facilitator will begin asking specific people to participate if a participant has the least amount of participation.

If participants do not have a response to a particular question, the Facilitator will step in and answer the question. If participants did not get enough participation points from this question-and-answer section, we can allow them to answer other questions from the session at the end as a revisitation.

To revisit a question requires them to have completed enough of their answers to share them and receive the required completion points. This might be useful for participants that did not complete enough of their questions before the group where the questions they did answer in the book were answered by other participants. Even if the participant did not complete a question before group, we can allow them to develop a quick answer on the spot if they are able.

Once the presentation process is over for the session, we allow the rest of the time to be open discussion starting with the facilitator asking the group if they have any questions, allowing participants to ask questions here. Next, we will do a check in, asking the group how they are doing with the concepts or fundamentals covered in the session. Once 2 hours have elapsed for session one, or three hours for all other sessions, the session is complete.

This is how the group will be Facilitated.

Continuum Groups – Level 2 Group

The continuum groups are meant for people who have already participated in a regular group and who have a desire to participate in a longer-term group. Also, in cases where a Facilitator does not have a Co-facilitator, they can provide Continuum Groups instead. If a Co-facilitator is available, we should always try to do the level 1 group first so that people who want either of the two certificates can get them and they can receive a reward or token from the group in the form of a certificate of participation (not of completion) or a coin (coins which we will make soon.) Level 2 groups will also provide a certificate or coin, however only after 52 sessions have been completed.

In this type of group, the Facilitator does not need to discuss participation requirements. Also, the first session will be given out as a packet of paper to any participants attending the group for the first time. By doing this, we skip session 1 and actually present material starting with session 2.

Sessions 2-5 will be broken down into 3 groups apiece. Instead of presenting all of the material for session 2, we will present the material for the concepts of Self-care, Recovery Planning, and Mentorship on three different days. We will separate the fundamentals from sessions 3-5 in the same way, tackling them in three days rather than in one.

The participants do not need to bring their books or read any slides. In this version of the group, the Facilitator reads everything. There is the introduction material starting with each concept or fundamental, followed by an inspirational passage, followed by asking the question "How does this passage relate to the 'concept' or 'fundamental.'

In asking this question, in the level 1 group, we like everyone to have already answered this question in their books and to read their response for the group. In this case, we ask them to answer the question spontaneously with the thoughts they have at the moment. This should ensure that even if they answer the question similarly each time, they may have noticed a connection today different from what they wrote in their books or answered in a previous level 2 group.

After this question, there are generally 3 questions asked that relate to the passage or recovery in general. These questions will also be answered spontaneously without the use of their book. These questions are usually something that they have experienced in more than one way and can provide different answers to each time they come across them.

Level 2 groups are meant to be an hour long. If the group runs shorter than this period, facilitators can do a check-in, asking how participants are experiencing the concept or fundamental in their lives. This group is meant to be continuous, thus the word Continuum in the name. While we will present the material in 12 weeks, people may want to continue them longer because with new participants being added consistently there should be diversity in how people answer questions over time.

This is how the group should be operated.

How to Become an RRPS Facilitator

To become an RRPS Facilitator, you must first, participate in an RRPS group. You cannot become a Facilitator for each of the different groups by only participating in one type of group. In order to qualify as a Facilitator of a specific group, a potential Facilitator has to participate in that specific group.

There are three different programs or groups. Radical Recovery Peer Support (RRPS), RRPS-University, and RRPS-Liberation. RRPS is for people who are experiencing general distress. RRPS-University is for people experiencing distress but who are either attempting a form of education beyond k-12, or who are thinking about doing so. RRPS-Liberation is for people with a criminal history that includes Driving Under the Influence.

At the present time, RRPS liberation training is only for potential Facilitators who have a criminal record or whose criminal records were expunged or pardoned. In the future, anyone can become an RRPS-Liberation Facilitator if they know another RRPS-Liberation facilitator, believe that the program is helping people with criminal records, and receive a written recommendation from an RRPS-Liberation Facilitator stating they believe you have the ability to work well with participants of this background or that they can attest that you have worked with this group of people before.

For RRPS-University, a Facilitator must show proof that they have at least 25 credits of college experience, or that they have received a certification in a particular skill and have worked in that field for 3 years.

For the RRPS program specifically, other than RRPS-University or RRPS-Liberation, there are no background requirements to become a Facilitator.

*After personally participating in a group, the Facilitation training will begin. Facilitation training involves working with an Advanced Level Co-Facilitator to present a group to 3 people (no more than 3). They will do this on a recorded Zoom session so the recording can be viewed to make sure the presentation process went smoothly. The low number of participants will ensure that the facilitator will also participate, as participation is divided among the participants and the Facilitators when the number of people attempting a certificate of completion is less than 5 persons.

For more information on how to divide the participation during a regular (non-training group) consult the text on page two of the Facilitator handbook. Or check out our blog titled "Participation Requirements" at www.communitypeerservices.com/blog This blog also states the amount of completion of the workbook needed by each person attempting to become a Facilitator.

During training, the potential Facilitator is not required to examine participants workbooks for completeness, this will be for their Advanced Level Co-facilitator to complete.

A potential Facilitator may need to find participants for their training group. We cannot guarantee that we will have willing participants. This means a Facilitator in training must find three people who want to get certified. We suggest trying to network with others in the mental health recovery, substance use recovery, or criminal Reentry fields such as Peer Supporters, or Forensic Peer Supporters via your social media.

The fee for participation in a group is $187.50 and the fee for the training opportunity is also $187.5. Payment plans are available upon request but for a higher overall price of $250.00 divided among 52 weeks. Anyone who does not pay their payment plans on time will have their certifications suspended. This means that they will not be able to provide certificates of completion that will be accepted by us, which means that the people participating in a group with a Facilitator who has been suspended will not be able to become facilitators and will need to do the group with a facilitator who is current with their payments.

**Once a person participates in a Facilitator training program, they are qualified to Facilitate any group without having to run a practice group for each (as long as background requirements are met). However, they will need to earn a certificate of completion for each group they want to Facilitate.

Author's note:

Hi, I am Dakota Fisher.

I designed this group because I believe in recovery. This will probably not be the only tool in your recovery toolbox, because a toolbox that has only one tool in it usually doesn't have much value. I hope that people participating in this program develop a system of recovery that works for them.

There are many systems of recovery that I participate in because my mind needs continual education concerning the issues I face. With respect to educating myself on these issues, I know that 1000 programs might never be enough to relieve me of an insanity that had at one time completely overtaken my ability to function productively and happily in society and my community.

My beliefs, thoughts, and feelings became twisted in a way that I could not see anything of value in the world and had become hopeless. No tool that I discovered had a complete answer because all of them were made by people who have different and unique views on recovery and had different experiences that helped them become thoughtful in specific areas.

Because no one has an exact recipe for how to help you recover, as only you can discover the mix of thoughts, beliefs, and feelings that work for you, it might be hard to find what is needed to begin and complete your recovery journey. In the worst instances, some of the people or programs we reach out to for help will try to convince us that their program is the best and that we should pick one above the others and commit to it.

From my perspective, one of the most important things in my recovery was not the programs themselves, but the people I would meet in a program that would become part of my support group. Having these people in my life helps me stay open-minded; moreover, it ensures that I usually have someone in recovery around me at all times, and if not, they are only a phone call away.

The way I see it, I need a diverse group of supporters, because each person in my circle only knows the part of the picture that they have experienced or been exposed to. A lot of times, people who are very knowledgeable about one thing do not have any valid answers to certain problems I have experienced. So, if one person doesn't have an answer, I need to find someone who does. This can only be accomplished by meeting them where they are at, wherever they are at.

In some cases, I will find that I can't entirely agree with a particular philosophy, or that a person who is supposed to be providing me with aid does not understand where I am coming from or why I feel the way I feel. I might sometimes be considering finding a new supporter. When this happens, I do not curse the whole program or field of care because of my bad experience. Most of the resources out there provide value to many people, or else they would not survive.

Therefore, it is important for me to carefully consider what it is about a program or person that I am in disagreement with and see if there is another option that will provide me with the best benefits that that program, service, or person offers. This might require a searching and fearless education into recovery resources to find out about their purpose, and their promises.

If I feel like something is not to my liking or is adversely affecting me, I want to have supporters, or trusted friends or family members who I can ask if they have noticed unpleasant changes or if they think I've been doing better. Sometimes it is hard for me to tell because I have had many intermingling problems that clouded my judgement. Having these people around will allow us to bring them to our appointments and explain what they are seeing in such cases where we want a change to be made but the person we are relying on to make the change doesn't listen to us or believe we are seeing clearly.

So, this program and education are both tools we might want in our toolbox. Other important "tools" or "resources" are having an open mind and having a willingness to experience new things. Open-mindedness and willingness will allow us to take advantage of the good aspects of any program and leave behind what doesn't work for us.

As a final note, one of the most pervasive and underlying concepts of this program is mentorship. The difference between mentorship and sponsorship is not so evident at first glance, but there are some distinguishing features. Sponsors of certain programs are indeed meant to practice the principles they have learned in all areas of their lives, but most people in this position will not be sponsors at work, school, or public places. They reserve their sponsorship for people with the particular issues that underlie their program of choice. A sponsor will usually not discuss issues that are outside of their primary area of concern. Some sponsors will say ambiguously that if we refrain from harmful behaviors everything will fall into place.

A Mentor will be a mentor in all places and for any issue. Mentors exhibit the best version of themselves in the work they do, in their field of study, in social and recreational settings, etc... Because we never know where we will meet a person that needs our help, we will try to live to our fullest potential so that when a person asks us how we handle situations with such grace, or where we find our motivation, we can tell them. Living our fullest potential will attract people to our way of life. Mentors will also be willing to talk about any facet of life with a person who is struggling even if they are not the best resource for that particular concern and will try to connect the person to someone with more insights if they find they cannot offer meaningful aid. We are always mentors, and our behavior will influence people for good or bad whether we know it does or not.

Authors Background

*United States Army Veteran

*BS Finance (honors)

*Current MBA student

*Pennsylvania - Certified Peer Specialist

*Forensic Peer Specialist

*MRT Facilitator

*Mental Health First Aider

**Formerly Incarcerated Person

References

- King, M. L., Jr. (1967, October 26). What Is Your Life's Blueprint? Barratt Junior High School in Philadelphia, Pennsylvania.
- King Jr., M. L. (1965, March 25). Keep Moving from This Mountain [Speech]. Spelman College, Atlanta, Georgia.

Prison Partnership Program (PPP)

Our goal is to have our group available at every prison in America. We can't do this without your help. If you work at a prison, visit our website www.communitypeerservices.com and click "contact" to reach out and find out how to become a Facilitator of our group.

Our intention is for the inmates themselves to work as Peer Supports in the prison and facilitate the groups themselves. However, we would need a staff member to oversee the group process to make sure the group is conducted appropriately.

IF YOUR CURRENTLY SERVING TIME IN PRISON – If your facility does not offer this group, we have a correspondence course available where you can earn a certificate that might help you be approved for parole. The more you work on your wellness, the better chance you have of reducing your sentence. Write to Community and Peer Services at 1016 Memorial Avenue, Williamsport, PA, 17701 to find out how to get involved in the program. Pass this along to others who might want to benefit from this opportunity who might not have heard of the program.

Experience the magic,

"Personal experiences and insights on recovery from a person in recovery – Innovative mental health workbooks that ask us insightful questions that help us make sense of complex issues of life."

www.communitypeerservices.com |

Experience the Insight.

"Personal experiences and insights on recovery from a person in recovery - Innovative mental health workbooks that ask us insightful questions that help us make sense of complex issues of life."

www.communitypeerservices.com |

Radical Recovery Peer Support Liberation

Community & Peer Services
Caps

Community & Peer Services
Caps

Community & Peer Services
Caps

To Explore Our Website go to

www.communitypeerservices.com

To learn more about our different group or training programs visit
www.communitypeerservices.com/blog

Find us on:
Facebook @ Community and Peer Services
LinkedIn @ Community and Peer Services
Twitter @2023caps
Reddit @ #RadicalRecovery
YouTube @ #RadicalRecovery